Microsoft Certified Azure Administrator

The Ultimate Guide to Practice Test Questions, Answers and Master the Associate Exam

Introduction

In today's ever-evolving digital landscape, cloud computing has become the linchpin of modern IT infrastructure. Organizations worldwide are embracing cloud services to harness the power of scalability, flexibility, and cost-efficiency. Among the leading cloud service providers, Microsoft Azure stands out as a dynamic and comprehensive platform, providing a wide array of services and solutions for businesses of all sizes.

As the demand for skilled Azure professionals continues to grow, the Microsoft Certified Azure Administrator Associate certification has become a coveted badge of expertise in the realm of cloud administration. This certification is a testament to an individual's competence in managing, maintaining, and securing Azure resources, making it a pivotal step for professionals aspiring to take their careers to new heights.

To conquer the Microsoft Certified Azure Administrator Associate exam and secure this valuable certification, you need comprehensive preparation. Practice makes perfect, and when it comes to the Microsoft Certified Azure Administrator Associate exam, practice tests are your best ally. This book offers a collection of meticulously crafted practice questions that cover every exam objective in detail. Whether you're a seasoned IT professional or a beginner, these practice tests will help you assess your knowledge, identify your strengths and weaknesses, and ultimately lead you to success in the certification exam.

A practice test is only as good as its answers, and that's why this book goes above and beyond to provide clear and detailed explanations for each question. We've taken care to ensure that every answer is not just correct but also thoroughly explained, giving you a deeper understanding of the concepts tested in the exam. With these answers at your disposal, you can learn from your mistakes, refine your knowledge, and build the expertise needed to pass the exam with confidence.

Beyond practice questions and answers, this book is designed to be a comprehensive study companion. We've structured the material to align with the Microsoft Certified Azure Administrator Associate exam objectives, ensuring that you're covering the topics most likely to be tested. Additionally, we've included tips, strategies, and insights from Azure experts to help you navigate the complexities of the exam and manage your time effectively.

What You'll Find Inside:

A comprehensive collection of practice questions covering all exam objectives.

Detailed and easy-to-understand answers with explanations to deepen your understanding.

Tips and strategies to help you optimize your study plan.

Real-world scenarios and best practices from experienced Azure administrators.

A roadmap to exam success, including registration and preparation tips.

Whether you're a seasoned IT professional looking to expand your skill set or someone taking their first steps in the world of cloud computing, this book is an invaluable resource that will help you attain the Microsoft Certified Azure Administrator Associate certification. With a strong foundation in Azure administration, you'll be well-equipped to tackle the challenges of managing and securing cloud resources, ensuring your place in the fast-paced world of modern IT.

Prepare to embark on a transformative journey that will elevate your career, open up new opportunities, and solidify your status as a Microsoft Certified Azure Administrator Associate.

Let's get started on your path to success in the world of Azure administration!

Who Should Buy This Book?

This study guide is designed for a wide range of individuals:

Aspiring Azure Administrators: If you are looking to start or advance your career in cloud administration and seek the Microsoft Certified: Azure Administrator certification, this book will serve as a valuable resource.

IT Professionals and Administrators: Current IT professionals and administrators who want to expand their knowledge and skillset to include Azure administration will find this guide invaluable.

Students and Learners: Students studying Azure or cloud computing in an educational setting can use this book to enhance their understanding and prepare for certification.

Self-Learners: Individuals who are passionate about Azure and prefer self-paced learning will find this book an excellent resource for mastering Azure administration.

Study Guide Features

Our study guide offers a range of features tailored to facilitate your journey to Azure Administrator certification success:

Exam Objectives

The book covers all exam objectives, ensuring that you are well-prepared for every topic that the AZ-104 exam may test you on. We provide in-depth explanations and examples to help you grasp the material.

Objective Map

A visual "Objective Map" illustrates the connections between different exam objectives, helping you understand how topics relate to one another. This map offers a strategic overview to guide your preparation.

Assessment Test

To evaluate your current knowledge and readiness for the AZ-104 exam, we've included an "Assessment Test." This test is designed to mirror the actual exam experience, with questions covering the full range of topics. It will help you identify areas where you need to focus your study efforts.

Answers to Assessment Test

A crucial aspect of any study guide is clarity in explanations. In this book, you'll find detailed answers and explanations for each question in the Assessment Test. These answers provide you with a deeper understanding of the material, ensuring that you learn from your mistakes and can improve your knowledge.

Whether you're new to Azure administration or looking to refine your existing skills, this study guide is your essential tool for success in the AZ-104: Microsoft Azure Administrator Exam. By the time you complete this guide, you'll be well-prepared to tackle the challenges of managing, maintaining, and securing Azure resources.

With the comprehensive coverage of exam objectives, visual aids to guide your study, and a thorough assessment test with detailed answers, you'll be in an excellent position to confidently achieve your Microsoft Certified: Azure Administrator certification. So, let's embark on your journey to success in Azure administration and gain the recognition and opportunities that come with it. Start your preparation with Microsoft Azure Administrator Exam Study Guide today!

Chapter 1: Identify: Azure Active Directory

In the vast and ever-evolving landscape of cloud computing, Microsoft Azure has firmly established itself as a prominent player. At the heart of Azure's identity and access management services is Azure Active Directory (Azure AD), a critical component that empowers organizations to secure their digital resources, manage user identities, and enable seamless collaboration. In this chapter, we will delve into the world of Azure AD, exploring its key features, components, and functionalities.

Azure Active Directory: The Foundation of Identity Management

Azure Active Directory is a comprehensive identity and access management solution provided by Microsoft. It serves as the backbone for authenticating and authorizing users and devices to access resources in the Azure cloud and within on-premises environments. Azure AD is at the core of securing data, applications, and services, making it a vital component for organizations embracing the cloud.

Key Features of Azure Active Directory:

User Identity Management: Azure AD allows you to create and manage user identities, providing them with secure access to various applications and services. This includes single sign-on (SSO) for a seamless user experience.

Group Management: Group management simplifies access control by allowing you to organize users into groups and assign permissions based on group memberships, streamlining administration.

Azure AD Roles: Azure AD roles define what users and administrators can do within the directory, including the ability to create, manage, or delegate various tasks.

Azure AD Join: Azure AD Join is the process of connecting devices to Azure AD, making it easier to manage device policies and settings.

Self-Service Password Reset: This feature empowers users to reset their passwords without IT intervention, reducing the burden on help desks and improving user productivity.

Managing Multiple Directories: Azure AD enables organizations to manage multiple directories from a single Azure AD tenant, streamlining the management of user identities across various domains and geographies.

Users and Groups in Azure Active Directory

User management is at the core of Azure Active Directory. Azure AD provides a centralized platform for creating, configuring, and managing user accounts. This user-centric approach enhances security and simplifies access control, making it an essential tool for administrators.

User Creation and Configuration:

Azure AD allows administrators to create and configure user accounts with specific attributes, roles, and access rights. Users can be associated with specific groups to simplify access management and permissions.

Group Management:

Groups are a fundamental part of user and access management in Azure AD. They provide a logical way to organize users and apply consistent access controls. Groups can be created for various purposes, such as departmental teams, project groups, or security roles. Group members inherit permissions based on their group memberships, streamlining access management.

Azure AD Roles: Defining Permissions

Azure AD roles are essential in defining and delegating permissions within the directory. These roles determine what actions users and administrators can perform in Azure AD. Azure AD offers various built-in roles, each tailored to specific tasks and responsibilities. Understanding and utilizing these roles is crucial for efficient access management.

Common Azure AD Roles:

Global Administrator: This role has full access to all administrative features in Azure AD, including user management, role assignments, and more. It's the highest level of privilege.

User Administrator: User administrators can create and manage user accounts and group memberships but don't have access to administrative features like billing or service settings.

Application Administrator: This role is focused on managing applications and their configurations, making it ideal for administrators responsible for application access.

Helpdesk Administrator: Helpdesk administrators can reset passwords and provide support to users, enhancing the efficiency of user support.

Security Administrator: Security administrators have access to security-related features in Azure AD, helping to ensure the safety of the directory.

Billing Administrator: Billing administrators can manage subscriptions and billing information, making them responsible for financial aspects of the directory.

Understanding and assigning roles is essential for delegating administrative tasks efficiently while maintaining security and compliance.

Azure AD Join: Connecting Devices

Azure AD Join is a crucial feature for organizations that need to manage device policies, settings, and access control efficiently. It facilitates the connection of devices to Azure AD, enabling organizations to enforce security policies, configure settings, and manage devices effectively.

Benefits of Azure AD Join:

Single Sign-On (SSO): Users can sign in to their devices and access resources with a single set of credentials, enhancing the user experience and simplifying access control.

Device Management: Azure AD Join allows administrators to enforce device policies, ensuring that devices meet security and compliance requirements.

Multi-Factor Authentication (MFA): MFA can be enabled to add an extra layer of security to device sign-ins, reducing the risk of unauthorized access.

Self-Service Password Reset: Users can reset their passwords if forgotten, reducing the burden on IT help desks.

By connecting devices to Azure AD, organizations can streamline the management of their digital assets while enhancing security and user experience.

Self-Service Password Reset: Empowering Users

One of the common challenges for IT departments is managing password resets. Azure AD offers a solution through self-service password reset, allowing users to reset their passwords without needing IT assistance. This feature not only saves time but also enhances user productivity and satisfaction.

Key Benefits of Self-Service Password Reset:

User Empowerment: Users can reset their own passwords, reducing reliance on IT support.

Time and Cost Savings: IT help desk teams spend less time on password-related requests, allowing them to focus on more critical tasks.

Increased Productivity: Users experience less downtime due to forgotten passwords, leading to higher productivity.

Security: Azure AD can enforce strong authentication methods during password reset, enhancing security.

User Verification: Self-service password reset may require users to answer security questions or use multifactor authentication to verify their identity.

Azure AD's self-service password reset feature strikes a balance between user convenience and security, resulting in a win-win for both IT departments and end-users.

Managing Multiple Directories

Organizations often operate multiple directories for different purposes, such as for various departments or geographic locations. Managing these directories efficiently can be challenging, but Azure AD simplifies this process by allowing you to manage multiple directories from a single Azure AD tenant.

Benefits of Managing Multiple Directories in Azure AD:

Centralized Management: Administrators can manage multiple directories from a single Azure AD tenant, streamlining user and access management.

Efficient Collaboration: Users from different directories can collaborate seamlessly, enhancing productivity and reducing friction.

Resource Sharing: Resources can be shared across directories, facilitating access to shared applications and data.

Improved Security: Azure AD's security features can be consistently applied across multiple directories, enhancing the overall security posture.

With the ability to manage multiple directories, organizations can maintain flexibility and scalability while centralizing administration and enhancing security. Understanding Azure AD's core features, user and group management, role assignments, Azure AD Join, self-service password reset, and the management of multiple directories is essential for anyone looking to navigate the Azure ecosystem efficiently. In subsequent chapters, we will delve deeper into each of these components, providing practical insights and guidance to empower you on your journey toward mastering Azure Active Directory and achieving success in cloud administration.

Exam Essentials

As you prepare for the Microsoft Certified: Azure Administrator Associate (AZ-104) or any certification exam related to Azure Active Directory (Azure AD), there are several essential concepts and best practices to keep in mind. In this section, we'll outline the key exam essentials for Azure AD, helping you focus your study efforts effectively and increasing your chances of success.

1. Understand Azure AD Core Concepts

User and Group Management: Be proficient in creating and managing user accounts and groups in Azure AD. This includes user attributes, group memberships, and the role of groups in access management.

Azure AD Roles: Familiarize yourself with the various built-in Azure AD roles, their permissions, and when to assign them. Roles play a significant role in access control and delegation.

Azure AD Join: Comprehend the process of connecting devices to Azure AD and the benefits it offers, such as single sign-on, device management, and self-service password reset.

Self-Service Password Reset: Understand how self-service password reset works and its advantages for both users and IT administrators.

Managing Multiple Directories: Learn how to manage multiple directories within a single Azure AD tenant, including the advantages of centralized administration and enhanced security.

2. Master Identity and Access Management

Identity Protection: Be aware of security features like Multi-Factor Authentication (MFA) and Conditional Access. Understand how to protect user identities and enforce security policies.

Directory Integration: Learn how to integrate on-premises directories with Azure AD using solutions like Azure AD Connect. This is crucial for hybrid identity scenarios.

Single Sign-On (SSO): Understand the benefits of SSO and how to configure it for various applications and services within Azure AD.

Access Control: Be able to configure access controls, permissions, and conditional access policies to ensure proper security and compliance.

3. Exam-Related Tasks

Practice with Real Scenarios: Utilize hands-on labs and real-world scenarios to gain practical experience in Azure AD administration. This will help you apply your knowledge effectively during the exam.

Review Official Documentation: Microsoft provides comprehensive documentation for Azure AD. Familiarize yourself with the official documentation to gain in-depth knowledge and troubleshooting tips.

Utilize Exam Resources: Take advantage of practice exams, study guides, and official Microsoft learning paths to assess your readiness and reinforce your understanding of exam topics.

4. Security and Compliance

Security Best Practices: Understand the best practices for securing Azure AD, including monitoring sign-in activities, configuring security alerts, and responding to security incidents.

Compliance and Auditing: Familiarize yourself with compliance requirements and auditing capabilities within Azure AD. Know how to manage audit logs and reports.

Data Protection: Be aware of data protection features, such as data loss prevention (DLP) policies and encryption, to safeguard sensitive information.

5. Troubleshooting and Problem Solving

Troubleshooting Skills: Develop strong troubleshooting skills to diagnose and resolve issues related to Azure AD, including sign-in problems, access issues, and connectivity errors.

Azure AD Connect Issues: Be prepared to troubleshoot synchronization issues if you are dealing with a hybrid identity scenario.

Testing and Validation: Know how to test and validate configurations before deploying changes in a production environment.

6. Stay Up-to-Date

Azure AD is an evolving platform with regular updates and new features. Stay informed about the latest changes and updates by following Microsoft's official Azure blog, attending webinars, and participating in community forums.

By focusing on these exam essentials for Azure Active Directory, you'll be well-prepared to tackle certification exams and succeed in managing Azure AD effectively. Remember that practical experience and hands-on practice are equally essential in reinforcing your knowledge and skills. Good luck with your Azure AD certification journey!

Review Questions

Review Questions ans Answers:

Question 1

You need to assign read-only access to a specific Azure Resource Group. Which built-in Role Based Access Control (RBAC) role should you assign?

A. Reader

B. Contributor

C. Owner

D. User

Answer: A.

The "Reader" role allows users to view resources within a resource group but not make any changes.

Question 2:

What is the purpose of Azure Resource Locks?

A. To secure your Azure subscription with a password.

B. To prevent users from deleting resources accidentally.

C. To restrict access to specific resources.

D. To limit the number of resources in a subscription.

Answer: B.

Azure Resource Locks are used to prevent accidental deletion or modification of resources within a subscription.

Question 3:

You want to ensure that Azure resources can be accessed only from specified IP addresses. What Azure service should you use?

A. Azure Firewall

B. Azure Load Balancer

C. Azure VPN Gateway

D. Azure Security Center

Answer: A.

Azure Firewall allows you to filter and control network traffic to and from resources based on source and destination IP addresses.

Question 4:

Which Azure service can be used to deploy virtual machines (VMs) in a highly available manner?

A. Azure Virtual Network

B. Azure Logic Apps

C. Azure Load Balancer

D. Azure DNS

Answer: C.

Azure Load Balancer can be used to distribute incoming traffic across multiple VM instances, ensuring high availability and fault tolerance.

Question 5:

You need to create a private network connection between your on-premises network and Azure. Which service should you use?

A. Azure ExpressRoute

B. Azure Virtual WAN

C. Azure VPN Gateway

D. Azure Site Recovery

Answer: A.

Azure ExpressRoute provides a dedicated private network connection between your on-premises data center and Azure.

Question 6:

You want to ensure that Azure virtual machines are automatically scaled based on performance metrics. What Azure service should you use?

A. Azure Logic Apps

B. Azure Autoscale

C. Azure Functions

D. Azure Virtual Network

Answer: B.

Azure Autoscale allows you to automatically adjust the number of VM instances based on performance metrics, ensuring optimal resource utilization.

Question 7:

Which Azure service is responsible for identity and access management within Azure?

A. Azure Active Directory (Azure AD)

B. Azure Functions

C. Azure Key Vault

D. Azure DevOps

Answer: A.

Azure Active Directory (Azure AD) is responsible for identity and access management within Azure.

Question 8:

You want to enable users to sign in to Azure services using their existing on-premises credentials. What Azure service should you use?

A. Azure Active Directory B2B

B. Azure AD Join

C. Azure AD Connect

D. Azure Multi-Factor Authentication

Answer: C.

Azure AD Connect is used to synchronize on-premises Active Directory with Azure Active Directory, allowing users to sign in using their existing credentials.

Question 9:

Which Azure service allows you to control access to resources based on user roles and permissions?

A. Azure Virtual Network

B. Azure Active Directory (Azure AD)

C. Azure Logic Apps

D. Azure App Service

Answer: B.

Azure Active Directory (Azure AD) is used for role-based access control (RBAC) and managing user roles and permissions.

Question 10:

You want to enable multi-factor authentication for additional security in Azure. Which Azure service should you use?

A. Azure Active Directory (Azure AD)

B. Azure Key Vault

C. Azure Security Center

D. Azure Logic Apps

Answer: A.

Azure Active Directory (Azure AD) offers Multi-Factor Authentication (MFA) for added security.

Question 11:

What is the purpose of Azure Policy?

A. To define resource properties for Azure resources.

B. To manage access control for Azure resources.

C. To enforce compliance with organizational standards and requirements.

D. To secure Azure resources using firewalls.

Answer: C.

Azure Policy is used to enforce compliance with organizational standards and requirements for Azure resources.

Question 12:

You need to ensure that sensitive information in Azure is encrypted at rest. What Azure service can you use for this purpose?

A. Azure Active Directory (Azure AD)

B. Azure Key Vault

C. Azure Information Protection

D. Azure Security Center

Answer: B.

Azure Key Vault provides encryption for sensitive information at rest.

Question 13:

You want to ensure that your Azure resources are monitored for security threats and vulnerabilities. Which Azure service should you use?

A. Azure Sentinel

B. Azure Logic Apps

C. Azure Active Directory (Azure AD)

D. Azure Functions

Answer: A.

Azure Sentinel is a cloud-native security information and event management (SIEM) service for monitoring threats and vulnerabilities.

Question 14:

Which Azure service can be used for continuous integration and continuous deployment (CI/CD) of applications?

A. Azure Logic Apps

B. Azure Functions

C. Azure DevOps

D. Azure Virtual Network

Answer: C.

Azure DevOps provides a comprehensive solution for CI/CD, enabling the automation of application deployment.

Question 15:

You want to create a serverless compute solution in Azure for running small pieces of code in response to events. What Azure service should you use?

A. Azure Logic Apps

B. Azure Functions

C. Azure Virtual Network

D. Azure App Service

Answer: B.

Azure Functions is a serverless compute service for running code in response to events.

Question 16:

Which Azure service can be used to monitor, troubleshoot, and optimize your application performance and availability?

A. Azure Application Insights

B. Azure Logic Apps

C. Azure AD Connect

D. Azure Virtual Network

Answer: A.

Azure Application Insights is used to monitor and troubleshoot application performance and availability.

Question 17:

You want to ensure that your Azure resources are backed up and can be recovered in case of data loss. What Azure service should you use?

A. Azure Logic Apps

B. Azure Backup

C. Azure Virtual Network

D. Azure Functions

Answer: B.

Azure Backup is used to back up and recover Azure resources.

Question 18:

You need to create a high-availability solution for your web application. What Azure service can be used to distribute incoming network traffic across multiple virtual machines?

A. Azure Functions

B. Azure Logic Apps

C. Azure Load Balancer

D. Azure VPN Gateway

Answer: C.

Azure Load Balancer distributes incoming network traffic across multiple virtual machines to ensure high availability.

Question 19:

Which Azure service provides a global network for building, deploying, and managing distributed applications?

A. Azure Application Gateway

B. Azure Virtual WAN

C. Azure AD Connect

D. Azure VPN Gateway

Answer: B.

Azure Virtual WAN provides a global network for building, deploying, and managing distributed applications.

Question 20:

You need to create a private network connection between your on-premises data center and Azure. What Azure service should you use?

A. Azure Logic Apps

B. Azure Virtual WAN

C. Azure VPN Gateway

D. Azure ExpressRoute

Answer: D.

Azure ExpressRoute provides a dedicated private network connection between your on-premises data center and Azure.

Question 21:

You want to ensure that your Azure resources can automatically scale based on performance metrics. What Azure service should you use?

A. Azure Functions

B. Azure Autoscale

C. Azure Logic Apps

D. Azure Virtual Network

Answer: B.

Azure Autoscale allows you to automatically adjust the number of resources based on performance metrics.

Question 22:

You need to enforce access control for your Azure resources and ensure that users are granted the minimum required permissions. What should you use for this purpose?

A. Azure Virtual Network

B. Azure Active Directory (Azure AD)

C. Azure Logic Apps

D. Azure AD Connect

Answer: B.

Azure Active Directory (Azure AD) is used for role-based access control (RBAC) to grant minimum required permissions.

Question 23:

Which Azure service allows you to control access to resources based on user roles and permissions?

A. Azure Virtual Network

B. Azure Functions

C. Azure Active Directory (Azure AD)

D. Azure App Service

Answer: C.

Azure Active Directory (Azure AD) is used for role-based access control (RBAC) to manage user roles and permissions.

Question 24:

You want to enable multi-factor authentication for enhanced security in Azure. What Azure service should you use?

A. Azure Active Directory (Azure AD)

B. Azure Key Vault

C. Azure Security Center

D. Azure Logic Apps

Answer: A.

Azure Active Directory (Azure AD) offers Multi-Factor Authentication (MFA) for enhanced security.

Question 25:

What is the purpose of Azure Policy?

A. To manage access control for Azure resources.

B. To define resource properties for Azure resources.

C. To secure Azure resources using firewalls.

D. To enforce compliance with organizational standards and requirements.

Answer: D.

Azure Policy is used to enforce compliance with organizational standards and requirements for Azure resources.

Question 26:

You need to ensure that sensitive information in Azure is encrypted at rest. What Azure service can you use for this purpose?

A. Azure Active Directory (Azure AD)

B. Azure Key Vault

C. Azure Information Protection

D. Azure Security Center

Answer: B.

Azure Key Vault provides encryption for sensitive information at rest.

Question 27:

You want to ensure that your Azure resources are monitored for security threats and vulnerabilities. Which Azure service should you use?

A. Azure Sentinel

B. Azure Logic Apps

C. Azure Active Directory (Azure AD)

D. Azure Functions

Answer: A.

Azure Sentinel is a cloud-native security information and event management (SIEM) service for monitoring threats and vulnerabilities.

Question 28:

Which Azure service can be used for continuous integration and continuous deployment (CI/CD) of applications?

A. Azure Logic Apps

B. Azure Functions

C. Azure DevOps

D. Azure Virtual Network

Answer: C.

Azure DevOps provides a comprehensive solution for CI/CD, enabling the automation of application deployment.

Question 29:

You want to create a serverless compute solution in Azure for running small pieces of code in response to events. What Azure service should you use?

A. Azure Logic Apps

B. Azure Functions

C. Azure Virtual Network

D. Azure App Service

Answer: B.

Azure Functions is a serverless compute service for running code in response to events.

Question 30:

Which Azure service can be used to monitor, troubleshoot, and optimize your application performance and availability?

A. Azure Application Insights

B. Azure Logic Apps

C. Azure AD Connect

D. Azure Virtual Network

Answer: A.

Azure Application Insights is used to monitor and troubleshoot application performance and availability.

Question 31:

You need to ensure that your Azure resources are backed up and can be recovered in case of data loss. What Azure service should you use?

A. Azure Logic Apps

B. Azure Backup

C. Azure Virtual Network

D. Azure Functions

Answer: B.

Azure Backup is used to back up and recover Azure resources.

Question 32:

You want to create a high-availability solution for your web application. What Azure service can be used to distribute incoming network traffic across multiple virtual machines?

A. Azure Functions

B. Azure Logic Apps

C. Azure Load Balancer

D. Azure VPN Gateway

Answer: C.

Azure Load Balancer distributes incoming network traffic across multiple virtual machines to ensure high availability.

Question 33:

Which Azure service provides a global network for building, deploying, and managing distributed applications?

A. Azure Application Gateway

B. Azure Virtual WAN

C. Azure AD Connect

D. Azure VPN Gateway

Answer: B.

Azure Virtual WAN provides a global network for building, deploying, and managing distributed applications.

Question 34:

You need to create a private network connection between your on-premises data center and Azure. What Azure service should you use?

A. Azure Logic Apps

B. Azure Virtual WAN

C. Azure VPN Gateway

D. Azure ExpressRoute

Answer: D.

Azure ExpressRoute provides a dedicated private network connection between your on-premises data center and Azure.

Question 35:

You want to ensure that your Azure resources can automatically scale based on performance metrics. What Azure service should you use?

A. Azure Functions

B. Azure Autoscale

C. Azure Logic Apps

D. Azure Virtual Network

Answer: B.

Azure Autoscale allows you to automatically adjust the number of resources based on performance metrics.

Question 36:

You need to enforce access control for your Azure resources and ensure that users are granted the minimum required permissions. What should you use for this purpose?

A. Azure Virtual Network

B. Azure Active Directory (Azure AD)

C. Azure Logic Apps

D. Azure AD Connect

Answer: B.

Azure Active Directory (Azure AD) is used for role-based access control (RBAC) to grant minimum required permissions.

Question 37:

Which Azure service allows you to control access to resources based on user roles and permissions?

A. Azure Virtual Network

B. Azure Functions

C. Azure Active Directory (Azure AD)

D. Azure App Service

Answer: C.

Azure Active Directory (Azure AD) is used for role-based access control (RBAC) to manage user roles and permissions.

Question 38:

You want to enable multi-factor authentication for enhanced security in Azure. What Azure service should you use?

A. Azure Active Directory (Azure AD)

B. Azure Key Vault

C. Azure Security Center

D. Azure Logic Apps

Answer: A.

Azure Active Directory (Azure AD) offers Multi-Factor Authentication (MFA) for enhanced security.

Chapter 2: Compliance and Cloud Governance

In the ever-expanding universe of cloud computing, organizations are increasingly adopting cloud services, and Microsoft Azure has emerged as a frontrunner in the cloud market. As businesses entrust their digital assets to the cloud, ensuring compliance, governance, and efficient resource management becomes paramount. In this chapter, we will explore essential concepts, tools, and best practices related to compliance and cloud governance within the Azure platform.

Azure Regions: The Geographic Footprint

Azure spans the globe with a network of data centers strategically located in regions worldwide. Azure regions are distinct geographic areas that host data centers equipped with a range of Azure services. These regions serve as the foundation for building resilient and geographically distributed cloud architectures.

Key Points to Consider:

Region Selection: Choosing the right Azure region for your workloads is crucial. Factors such as data residency, latency, and disaster recovery should guide your selection.

Availability Zones: Azure regions often consist of multiple Availability Zones, providing redundancy and fault tolerance. Understanding and leveraging these zones is essential for high availability.

Data Residency and Compliance: Azure regions are critical in addressing data residency requirements and ensuring compliance with regional data protection laws.

Azure Accounts and Subscriptions: The Hierarchy

Azure follows a hierarchical structure that begins with Azure accounts, which are associated with Microsoft identities, and encompasses subscriptions that group resources together for billing and management purposes.

Key Components:

Azure Account: An Azure account represents the identity associated with Azure services. It can be an individual's Microsoft account or a work or school account.

Azure Subscription: A subscription is a billing container that organizes and isolates Azure resources. Organizations can have multiple subscriptions to separate costs, resources, and access control.

Subscription Management: Proper subscription management is essential for efficient resource allocation, billing, and access control. It's important to understand the relationships between accounts and subscriptions.

Azure Cost Management: Controlling Expenditure

Managing cloud costs is a vital aspect of cloud governance. Azure Cost Management offers tools and capabilities to monitor, optimize, and control your spending within Azure.

Cost Management Features:

Cost Tracking: Azure Cost Management provides detailed cost reports, usage tracking, and forecasting to help you understand where your cloud budget is going.

Budget Alerts: Create budget alerts to receive notifications when your spending approaches predefined thresholds.

Resource Optimization: Analyze resource costs and identify opportunities for cost savings. Azure Advisor provides recommendations for resource optimization.

Resource Groups: Logical Resource Organization

Resource Groups are logical containers that help organize and manage Azure resources. They enable you to group related resources together, making it easier to apply policies, security settings, and cost management strategies.

Resource Group Best Practices:

Naming Conventions: Implement consistent naming conventions for resource groups to facilitate organization and management.

Resource Tagging: Utilize resource tagging to categorize resources and enable better cost allocation and reporting.

Policy Enforcement: Apply Azure Policy at the resource group level to enforce governance rules consistently.

Azure Policy: Governance and Compliance

Azure Policy is a powerful tool for enforcing organizational standards and compliance in Azure environments. It allows you to define and apply rules and restrictions across resources.

Key Azure Policy Features:

Custom Policies: Create custom policies to match your organization's specific compliance requirements.

Policy Assignments: Assign policies to resource groups or subscriptions to enforce governance at various levels.

Compliance Reporting: Monitor and report on policy compliance to ensure resources adhere to defined rules.

Role-Based Access Control (RBAC): Fine-Grained Access Control

RBAC is essential for defining who can access Azure resources and what they can do with them. It allows for precise role assignment, ensuring that only authorized individuals have specific permissions.

RBAC Roles:

Owner: Has full access to all resources within a subscription, including the ability to delegate access to others.

Contributor: Can create and manage resources but cannot grant access to others.

Reader: Has read-only access and cannot make any changes to resources.

Custom Roles: Azure allows the creation of custom roles tailored to specific needs.

Resource Locks: Preventing Accidental Deletions

Resource Locks are crucial for protecting resources from accidental deletions or modifications. They come in two types: Delete and Read-only, and they prevent unauthorized changes.

Use Cases for Resource Locks:

Preventing Deletions: Apply a Delete lock to critical resources to prevent them from being accidentally deleted.

Ensuring Compliance: Apply Read-only locks to resources that should not be modified to maintain compliance.

Management Control: Resource locks are especially useful in production environments to safeguard critical resources.

Resource Tags: Categorizing Resources

Resource tagging is a powerful way to categorize and organize resources for easier management, billing, and reporting. Tags allow you to assign metadata to resources based on criteria that matter to your organization.

Benefits of Resource Tagging:

Cost Allocation: Tags enable more accurate cost allocation, helping you identify the cost of specific projects or departments.

Management: Use tags to filter and manage resources efficiently.

Reporting: Tags are valuable for creating custom reports and dashboards based on your organization's needs.

Azure's compliance and cloud governance tools and best practices play a pivotal role in managing resources effectively, optimizing costs, and ensuring compliance with organizational and regulatory requirements. Understanding Azure regions, the account-subscription hierarchy, cost management, resource groups, Azure Policy, RBAC, resource locks, and resource tagging is essential for successful Azure administration and governance. The proper implementation of these concepts will help organizations harness the full potential of Azure while maintaining control, security, and efficiency in their cloud environments.

Exam Essentials for Compliance and Cloud Governance

As you prepare for the Microsoft Certified: Azure Administrator Associate (AZ-104) or any certification exam related to Azure compliance and cloud governance, it's important to grasp key concepts, tools, and best practices. These essentials will help you demonstrate your expertise in managing Azure resources while adhering to compliance standards and optimizing cloud governance.

1. Azure Regions and Data Residency

Understand Azure Regions: Be familiar with the concept of Azure regions, their geographic distribution, and how they relate to data residency and disaster recovery.

Compliance Implications: Know how region selection impacts compliance with data protection laws and regional regulations.

Availability Zones: Learn the significance of Availability Zones within Azure regions for ensuring high availability and fault tolerance.

2. Azure Accounts and Subscriptions

Azure Account Types: Differentiate between Microsoft accounts, work or school accounts, and organizational accounts associated with Azure.

Subscriptions: Understand the role of Azure subscriptions as billing containers, and the reasons for creating multiple subscriptions.

Billing and Access Control: Know how Azure subscriptions are used for billing, resource organization, and access control.

3. Azure Cost Management

Cost Tracking: Master the tools and reports available for tracking and monitoring costs within Azure Cost Management.

Budget Alerts: Understand how to set budget alerts to control cloud expenditure and prevent overspending.

Resource Optimization: Learn how to identify cost-saving opportunities through resource optimization recommendations.

4. Resource Groups

Resource Group Organization: Grasp the role of resource groups in logically organizing and managing Azure resources.

Naming Conventions: Implement consistent naming conventions to enhance resource group organization and management.

Resource Tagging: Utilize resource tagging to categorize and manage resources efficiently, enabling cost allocation and reporting.

5. Azure Policy

Azure Policy Essentials: Comprehend the purpose and capabilities of Azure Policy in enforcing governance rules and compliance standards.

Custom Policies: Learn to create custom policies tailored to your organization's specific compliance requirements.

Policy Assignments: Know how to assign policies to resource groups or subscriptions to enforce governance across different levels of your Azure environment.

6. Role-Based Access Control (RBAC)

Role Assignments: Understand the different built-in roles (e.g., Owner, Contributor, Reader) and their associated permissions.

Custom Roles: Familiarize yourself with the process of creating custom roles to match specific organizational needs.

Least Privilege Principle: Apply the principle of least privilege by assigning roles that provide only the necessary permissions to individuals or groups.

7. Resource Locks

Resource Lock Types: Differentiate between Delete and Read-only locks and their use cases in safeguarding Azure resources.

Accidental Deletion Prevention: Learn how to apply Delete locks to critical resources to prevent accidental deletions.

Compliance and Security: Understand the role of Read-only locks in maintaining compliance and security of resources that should not be modified.

8. Resource Tags

Resource Tagging Benefits: Recognize the advantages of resource tagging for cost allocation, management, and reporting.

Cost Allocation: Understand how tags enable accurate cost allocation and identification of the cost of specific projects or departments.

Filtering and Reporting: Use tags for filtering and efficient resource management, and creating custom reports and dashboards.

By focusing on these exam essentials, you'll be well-prepared to excel in compliance and cloud governance topics during your certification exam. Practical experience and hands-on practice with Azure governance tools will also be instrumental in reinforcing your knowledge and skills. These essentials will not only aid in exam success but also prove valuable in effectively managing Azure resources in real-world scenarios.

Review questions and answers

Question 1:

You need to ensure that only a specific set of users can delete Azure resources while others are restricted from deleting resources. What should you use?

A. Azure Policies

B. Role-Based Access Control (RBAC)

C. Resource Locks

D. Custom Tags

Answer: C. Resource Locks

Question 2:

Which Azure tool helps you monitor, allocate costs, and set budget alerts for your cloud resources?

A. Azure Monitor

B. Azure Policy

C. Azure Cost Management

D. Azure Log Analytics

Answer: C. Azure Cost Management

Question 3:

You want to ensure that all resources in a specific resource group are compliant with your organization's naming conventions. What Azure service should you use?

A. Azure Monitor

B. Azure Policy

C. Role-Based Access Control (RBAC)

D. Azure AD

Answer: B. Azure Policy

Question 4:

What is the primary purpose of Azure Resource Groups?

A. To assign roles to users

B. To create custom policies

C. To organize and manage Azure resources

D. To enforce data protection regulations

Answer: C. To organize and manage Azure resources

Question 5:

You need to ensure that a specific user can read, but not modify, Azure resources. Which Role-Based Access Control (RBAC) role should you assign?

A. Owner

B. Contributor

C. Reader

D. Resource Lock

Answer: C. Reader

Question 6:

Which Azure service helps prevent accidental deletions of critical resources?

A. Azure Policy

B. Role-Based Access Control (RBAC)

C. Resource Locks

D. Azure Monitor

Answer: C. Resource Locks

Question 7:

Azure Regions are essential for what aspect of cloud governance?

A. Data residency

B. Budget alerts

C. Cost optimization

D. Role assignment

Answer: A. Data residency

Question 8:

Which Azure service allows you to create custom governance policies for your cloud resources?

A. Azure Monitor

B. Azure Policy

C. Azure Resource Groups

D. Azure Cost Management

Answer: B. Azure Policy

Question 9:

You need to allocate costs accurately to specific projects in your organization. What Azure feature should you utilize?

A. Azure Resource Groups

B. Azure Cost Management

C. Role-Based Access Control (RBAC)

D. Resource Locks

Answer: B. Azure Cost Management

Question 10:

What is the role of Azure Accounts in the context of Azure cloud governance?

A. To organize resources

B. To enforce policies

C. To manage access control

D. To represent user identities

Answer: D. To represent user identities

Question 11:

You are responsible for managing Azure resources for different departments in your organization. What Azure concept should you use to separate their costs and access control?

A. Azure Resource Groups

B. Azure Accounts

C. Azure Subscriptions

D. Azure Policies

Answer: C. Azure Subscriptions

Question 12:

You want to create a governance rule that enforces specific compliance standards for your organization's Azure resources. What Azure service should you use?

A. Azure Resource Groups

B. Azure Cost Management

C. Azure Policy

D. Role-Based Access Control (RBAC)

Answer: C. Azure Policy

Question 13:

You need to ensure that only specific users have full control over Azure resources, including the ability to delegate access to others. What Role-Based Access Control (RBAC) role should you assign?

A. Owner

B. Contributor

C. Reader

D. Custom Role

Answer: A. Owner

Question 14:

What is the primary purpose of Resource Locks in Azure?

A. To enforce compliance standards

B. To protect resources from unauthorized access

C. To prevent accidental deletions or modifications

D. To allocate costs to specific projects

Answer: C. To prevent accidental deletions or modifications

Question 15:

You want to organize Azure resources efficiently and improve cost allocation. What Azure feature should you use?

A. Azure Cost Management

B. Azure Resource Groups

C. Azure Policy

D. Role-Based Access Control (RBAC)

Answer: B. Azure Resource Groups

Question 16:

Which Azure concept allows you to create custom roles with specific permissions tailored to your organization's needs?

A. Azure Policies

B. Azure Resource Groups

C. Role-Based Access Control (RBAC)

D. Custom Tags

Answer: C. Role-Based Access Control (RBAC)

Question 17:

You need to ensure that specific users have read-only access to Azure resources without the ability to make changes. What Role-Based Access Control (RBAC) role should you assign?

A. Owner

B. Contributor

C. Reader

D. Custom Role

Answer: C. Reader

Question 18:

Which Azure feature allows you to categorize resources for cost allocation and reporting purposes?

A. Azure Policies

B. Azure Resource Groups

C. Role-Based Access Control (RBAC)

D. Resource Tags

Answer: D. Resource Tags

Question 19:

You want to ensure that critical resources are protected from accidental deletions or modifications. What Azure feature should you use?

A. Azure Policy

B. Azure Cost Management

C. Resource Locks

D. Role-Based Access Control (RBAC)

Answer: C. Resource Locks

Question 20:

You need to create governance rules for enforcing specific compliance standards within your Azure environment. What Azure service should you use?

A. Azure Monitor

B. Azure Cost Management

C. Azure Policy

D. Azure Resource Groups

Answer: C. Azure Policy

Question 21:

What is the primary role of Azure Accounts in the context of Azure cloud governance?

A. To organize and manage resources

B. To enforce governance policies

C. To represent user identities

D. To allocate costs

Answer: C. To represent user identities

Question 22:

You are responsible for managing Azure resources for different departments in your organization. What Azure concept should you use to separate their costs, resources, and access control?

A. Azure Resource Groups

B. Azure Subscriptions

C. Azure Accounts

D. Azure Policies

Answer: B. Azure Subscriptions

Question 23:

You want to create and enforce governance rules that ensure resources adhere to specific compliance standards. What Azure service should you use?

A. Azure Cost Management

B. Azure Policy

C. Role-Based Access Control (RBAC)

D. Resource Locks

Answer: B. Azure Policy

Question 24:

You need to ensure that a specific user can fully control Azure resources, including the ability to delegate access to others. What Role-Based Access Control (RBAC) role should you assign?

A. Owner

B. Contributor

C. Reader

D. Custom Role

Answer: A. Owner

Question 25:

What is the primary purpose of Resource Locks in Azure?

A. To allocate costs to specific projects

B. To prevent accidental deletions or modifications

C. To protect resources from unauthorized access

D. To enforce compliance standards

Answer: B. To prevent accidental deletions or modifications

Question 26:

You want to organize Azure resources efficiently and enhance cost allocation. What Azure feature should you use?

A. Azure Resource Groups

B. Azure Cost Management

C. Role-Based Access Control (RBAC)

D. Azure Policies

Answer: A. Azure Resource Groups

Question 27:

Which Azure concept enables you to create custom roles with specific permissions tailored to your organization's needs?

A. Azure Policies

B. Azure Resource Groups

C. Role-Based Access Control (RBAC)

D. Custom Tags

Answer: C. Role-Based Access Control (RBAC)

Question 28:

You need to ensure that specific users have read-only access to Azure resources without the ability to make changes. What Role-Based Access Control (RBAC) role should you assign?

A. Owner

B. Contributor

C. Reader

D. Custom Role

Answer: C. Reader

Question 29:

Which Azure feature allows you to categorize resources for cost allocation and reporting purposes?

A. Azure Policies

B. Azure Resource Groups

C. Role-Based Access Control (RBAC)

D. Resource Tags

Answer: D. Resource Tags

Question 30:

You want to protect critical resources from accidental deletions or modifications. What Azure feature should you use?

A. Azure Policy

B. Azure Cost Management

C. Resource Locks

D. Role-Based Access Control (RBAC)

Answer: C. Resource Locks

Question 31:

You need to create governance rules for enforcing specific compliance standards within your Azure environment. What Azure service should you use?

A. Azure Monitor

B. Azure Cost Management

C. Azure Policy

D. Azure Resource Groups

Answer: C. Azure Policy

Question 32:

What is the primary role of Azure Accounts in the context of Azure cloud governance?

A. To organize and manage resources

B. To enforce governance policies

C. To represent user identities

D. To allocate costs

Answer: C. To represent user identities

Question 33:

You are responsible for managing Azure resources for different departments in your organization. What Azure concept should you use to separate their costs, resources, and access control?

A. Azure Resource Groups

B. Azure Subscriptions

C. Azure Accounts

D. Azure Policies

Answer: B. Azure Subscriptions

Question 34:

You want to create and enforce governance rules that ensure resources adhere to specific compliance standards. What Azure service should you use?

A. Azure Cost Management

B. Azure Policy

C. Role-Based Access Control (RBAC)

D. Resource Locks

Answer: B. Azure Policy

Question 35:

You need to ensure that a specific user can fully control Azure resources, including the ability to delegate access to others. What Role-Based Access Control (RBAC) role should you assign?

A. Owner

B. Contributor

C. Reader

D. Custom Role

Answer: A. Owner

Question 36:

What is the primary purpose of Resource Locks in Azure?

A. To allocate costs to specific projects

B. To prevent accidental deletions or modifications

C. To protect resources from unauthorized access

D. To enforce compliance standards

Answer: B. To prevent accidental deletions or modifications

Question 37:

You want to organize Azure resources efficiently and enhance cost allocation. What Azure feature should you use?

A. Azure Resource Groups

B. Azure Cost Management

C. Role-Based Access Control (RBAC)

D. Azure Policies

Answer: A. Azure Resource Groups

Question 38:

Which Azure concept enables you to create custom roles with specific permissions tailored to your organization's needs?

A. Azure Policies

B. Azure Resource Groups

C. Role-Based Access Control (RBAC)

D. Custom Tags

Answer: C. Role-Based Access Control (RBAC)

Question 39:

You need to ensure that specific users have read-only access to Azure resources without the ability to make changes. What Role-Based Access Control (RBAC) role should you assign?

A. Owner

B. Contributor

C. Reader

D. Custom Role

Answer: C. Reader

Question 40:

Which Azure feature allows you to categorize resources for cost allocation and reporting purposes?

A. Azure Policies

B. Azure Resource Groups

C. Role-Based Access Control (RBAC)

D. Resource Tags

Answer: D. Resource Tags

Question 41:

You want to protect critical resources from accidental deletions or modifications. What Azure feature should you use?

A. Azure Policy

B. Azure Cost Management

C. Resource Locks

D. Role-Based Access Control (RBAC)

Answer: C. Resource Locks

Question 42:

You need to create governance rules for enforcing specific compliance standards within your Azure environment. What Azure service should you use?

A. Azure Monitor

B. Azure Cost Management

C. Azure Policy

D. Azure Resource Groups

Answer: C. Azure Policy

Question 43:

What is the primary role of Azure Accounts in the context of Azure cloud governance?

A. To organize and manage resources

B. To enforce governance policies

C. To represent user identities

D. To allocate costs

Answer: C. To represent user identities

Question 44:

You are responsible for managing Azure resources for different departments in your organization. What Azure concept should you use to separate their costs, resources, and access control?

A. Azure Resource Groups

B. Azure Subscriptions

C. Azure Accounts

D. Azure Policies

Answer: B. Azure Subscriptions

Question 45:

You want to create and enforce governance rules that ensure resources adhere to specific compliance standards. What Azure service should you use?

A. Azure Cost Management

B. Azure Policy

C. Role-Based Access Control (RBAC)

D. Resource Locks

Answer: B. Azure Policy

Chapter 3: Virtual Networking

In the realm of cloud computing, one of the foundational components that underpins the functionality of cloud services is virtual networking. Microsoft Azure, as a leading cloud platform, provides a robust and flexible virtual networking infrastructure that enables organizations to establish and manage their network architecture in the cloud. In this chapter, we will dive deep into the world of virtual networking within Azure, covering essential concepts, IP addressing, routing, security, and more.

Virtual Networks: The Building Blocks

Azure Virtual Networks (VNets) serve as the fundamental building blocks for constructing cloud-based network infrastructure. They provide isolation and segmentation of network resources, facilitating the organization's network design.

Key Aspects of Azure Virtual Networks:

Isolation: VNets isolate resources, creating network boundaries for enhanced security and network control.

Subnets: VNets consist of one or more subnets, which further segment resources within the VNet.

Connectivity: VNets enable connectivity between resources, extending on-premises networks to the cloud or connecting VNets.

VNet Concepts: Address Spaces and Peering

Understanding VNet concepts is essential for designing a well-structured network architecture. This includes IP address spaces, VNet peering, and various connectivity scenarios.

VNet Concepts in Detail:

IP Addressing: Define IP address spaces for VNets and subnets, ensuring efficient IP allocation and collision prevention.

VNet Peering: Create connections between VNets to enable resource sharing while maintaining isolation.

Transit and Gateway VNets: Utilize transit VNets and gateway VNets for more complex network scenarios.

IP Addressing: The Foundation of Networking

IP addressing is the backbone of networking, and in Azure, it plays a crucial role in resource identification, communication, and routing. Understanding IP addressing is fundamental to Azure virtual networking.

IP Addressing in Azure:

Private IP Addresses: Azure resources within a VNet are assigned private IP addresses for internal communication.

Public IP Addresses: Public IP addresses are used for resources that require public internet access.

Dynamic and Static IPs: Azure allows both dynamic and static IP assignment to resources.

Network Routes: Directing Traffic

Network routes define how traffic is directed within a virtual network. By managing routing, administrators can control how data flows between subnets and resources.

Routing Essentials:

System Routes: Azure creates default system routes to handle local traffic and direct traffic to the internet or VPN gateways.

User-Defined Routes: Administrators can create custom routes to guide traffic within the VNet and to external destinations.

Effective Routes: Understand how effective routes are determined by the combination of system and user-defined routes.

Service Endpoints: Secure and Optimized Access

Azure Service Endpoints enhance security and optimize data flow to Azure services by enabling private and direct connections.

Key Points:

Azure Service Endpoints: Service endpoints allow resources within a VNet to connect directly to Azure services over a private connection, bypassing the public internet.

Security and Performance: By utilizing service endpoints, organizations can improve security by keeping traffic within the Azure backbone and enhance performance.

Private Endpoint: Isolating Resources

Private endpoints are essential for securely accessing Azure services while maintaining network isolation. They allow resources in a VNet to privately connect to PaaS services without exposing them to the public internet.

Private Endpoint Highlights:

Isolation and Security: Private endpoints isolate Azure services and provide an additional layer of security for data traffic.

Supported Services: Various Azure services, such as Azure SQL Database and Azure Storage, support private endpoints.

Configuring Private Endpoints: Learn how to configure and manage private endpoints for Azure services.

Azure DNS: DNS Management in Azure

Azure DNS provides a reliable, secure, and scalable domain name system (DNS) service in the cloud, allowing organizations to manage DNS records and resolve hostnames.

Key Aspects of Azure DNS:

Domain Management: Create and manage DNS zones, records, and aliases in Azure DNS.

Integration: Integrate Azure DNS with your virtual networks for efficient DNS resolution.

Security: Ensure secure DNS management through role-based access control and access policies.

Network Security Groups (NSGs): Traffic Filtering

Network Security Groups are a critical component for controlling inbound and outbound traffic to network resources, providing security at the network level.

NSG Functionality:

Rule-Based Filtering: Configure NSG rules to allow or deny traffic based on source, destination, and port.

Associating NSGs: Associate NSGs with subnets or individual resources for granular control.

Default Rules: Understand default NSG rules, such as the default deny-all rule and the importance of rule evaluation order.

Azure Firewall: Centralized Network Security

Azure Firewall acts as a central security service, providing network-level protection for resources within a VNet. It allows for application and network-level filtering and threat protection.

Azure Firewall Essentials:

Network and Application Rules: Define rules to permit or deny traffic, both at the network and application levels.

Threat Intelligence: Leverage Azure Firewall's threat intelligence to enhance security against known threats.

Integration: Integrate Azure Firewall with VNets and route traffic through it for comprehensive network security.

Virtual networking is the backbone of any cloud-based infrastructure, and mastering the intricacies of Azure virtual networking is essential for effective cloud management and security. By understanding VNet concepts, IP addressing, network routes, service endpoints, private endpoints, Azure DNS, Network Security Groups (NSGs), and Azure Firewall, organizations can design, implement, and maintain a robust and secure network architecture within the Azure cloud environment. These concepts are vital not only for exam success but also for ensuring the efficient operation of Azure resources and the protection of data and applications in a cloud environment.

Exam Essentials for Virtual Networking

As you prepare for Microsoft Azure certification exams, including the Microsoft Certified: Azure Administrator Associate (AZ-104) or those focused on virtual networking, it's important to master key concepts and best practices related to virtual networking in Azure. These essentials will help you demonstrate your expertise in designing, configuring, and managing virtual networks within the Azure environment.

1. Azure Virtual Networks (VNets)

Understanding VNet Fundamentals: Grasp the core concepts of Azure Virtual Networks, such as isolation, subnets, and their role in creating network boundaries.

Connectivity: Understand how VNets enable connectivity between resources, both within the VNet and between VNets, including options for extending on-premises networks.

Transit and Gateway VNets: Learn about transit VNets and gateway VNets, which are crucial for more complex network scenarios, such as hub-and-spoke architectures and connecting to on-premises networks.

2. IP Addressing and Subnets

IP Address Allocation: Familiarize yourself with IP address allocation within VNets, including private IP addresses assigned to resources for internal communication.

Public IP Addresses: Understand the role of public IP addresses for resources that require public internet access.

Dynamic and Static IPs: Learn how to assign both dynamic and static IP addresses to resources based on your specific requirements.

3. Network Routing

System Routes: Recognize the role of system routes, including default routes that handle local traffic, traffic to the internet, and VPN gateways.

User-Defined Routes: Learn how to create custom routes to guide traffic within the VNet, such as directing traffic to specific next hops or enforcing network policies.

Effective Routes: Understand how effective routes are determined by a combination of system routes and user-defined routes.

4. Azure Service Endpoints

Private Connections to Azure Services: Understand the purpose of Azure Service Endpoints, which allow resources within a VNet to connect directly to Azure services over a private connection, enhancing security and performance.

Security and Optimization: Learn how service endpoints improve security by keeping traffic within the Azure backbone and optimize data flow to Azure services.

5. Private Endpoints

Secure Resource Access: Grasp the importance of private endpoints for securely accessing Azure services while maintaining network isolation.

Resource Types Supporting Private Endpoints: Familiarize yourself with Azure services that support private endpoints, such as Azure SQL Database and Azure Storage.

Configuration and Management: Learn how to configure and manage private endpoints for supported Azure services.

6. Azure DNS

DNS Management: Understand the role of Azure DNS in providing domain name system (DNS) services in the cloud, allowing the management of DNS zones, records, and aliases.

Integration with VNets: Learn how to integrate Azure DNS with virtual networks to ensure efficient DNS resolution for Azure resources.

Security and Access Control: Ensure secure DNS management by implementing role-based access control and access policies.

7. Network Security Groups (NSGs)

Traffic Filtering and Security: Recognize the importance of Network Security Groups in controlling inbound and outbound traffic to network resources and enhancing security at the network level.

Rule-Based Filtering: Learn how to configure NSG rules to allow or deny traffic based on source, destination, and port.

Associating NSGs: Understand how to associate NSGs with subnets or individual resources to gain granular control over network traffic.

8. Azure Firewall

Centralized Network Security: Comprehend the role of Azure Firewall in providing network-level protection for resources within a VNet, including application and network-level filtering and threat protection.

Network and Application Rules: Learn how to define rules within Azure Firewall to permit or deny traffic, both at the network and application levels.

Threat Intelligence: Utilize Azure Firewall's threat intelligence to enhance security by protecting against known threats.

Integration and Route Traffic: Understand how to integrate Azure Firewall with VNets and route traffic through it to ensure comprehensive network security.

By focusing on these exam essentials for virtual networking in Azure, you'll be well-prepared to excel in this domain during your certification exam. Practical experience, hands-on labs, and real-world practice with Azure networking tools are equally crucial in reinforcing your knowledge and skills. These essentials will not only aid in exam success but also prove invaluable in effectively designing and managing virtual networks in the Azure cloud environment.

Review Questions and Answers

Question 1:

You want to create a private connection between an Azure virtual network and Azure SQL Database for enhanced security. What feature should you use?

A. Azure VPN Gateway

B. Azure ExpressRoute

C. Azure Service Endpoint

D. Azure Private Endpoint

Answer: D. Azure Private Endpoint

Question 2:

What is the purpose of Azure Service Endpoints?

A. To allow public internet access to Azure services

B. To establish private connections from an Azure virtual network to Azure services

C. To create virtual network peering

D. To manage DNS settings for Azure resources

Answer: B. To establish private connections from an Azure virtual network to Azure services

Question 3:

Which Azure networking component enables you to control inbound and outbound traffic to network resources by defining rules based on source, destination, and port?

A. Azure Firewall

B. Azure DNS

C. Network Security Groups (NSGs)

D. Resource Locks

Answer: C. Network Security Groups (NSGs)

Question 4:

What is the primary function of Azure DNS in the Azure environment?

A. To provide cloud-based firewall and threat protection

B. To assign IP addresses to Azure virtual machines

C. To manage domain name system (DNS) services for Azure resources

D. To create virtual network peering

Answer: C. To manage domain name system (DNS) services for Azure resources

Question 5:

You need to connect multiple Azure virtual networks, allowing them to communicate with each other. What feature should you configure?

A. Azure Resource Manager

B. Azure Traffic Manager

C. Azure VNet Peering

D. Azure ExpressRoute

Answer: C. Azure VNet Peering

Question 6:

In Azure, what is the primary purpose of an IP address?

A. To allocate storage for virtual machines

B. To manage domain name system (DNS) settings

C. To identify and locate resources in a virtual network

D. To configure network security group rules

Answer: C. To identify and locate resources in a virtual network

Question 7:

What is the primary function of a system route in Azure virtual networking?

A. To define custom routes for network traffic

B. To route traffic to the internet

C. To control inbound traffic to virtual machines

D. To handle local traffic within the virtual network

Answer: D. To handle local traffic within the virtual network

Question 8:

You want to ensure that only a specific set of users can delete Azure resources while others are restricted from deleting resources. What should you use?

A. Azure Policies

B. Role-Based Access Control (RBAC)

C. Resource Locks

D. Custom Tags

Answer: C. Resource Locks

Question 9:

Which Azure component allows for centralized network-level protection and filtering of traffic for resources within a virtual network?

A. Azure VPN Gateway

B. Azure ExpressRoute

C. Azure Firewall

D. Azure Traffic Manager

Answer: C. Azure Firewall

Question 10:

What is the primary purpose of a private endpoint in Azure?

A. To enable public internet access to Azure services

B. To establish secure, private connections to Azure services

C. To configure domain name system (DNS) settings for virtual networks

D. To create network security group rules

Answer: B. To establish secure, private connections to Azure services

Question 11:

You need to allow a virtual machine in Azure to have public internet access. What type of IP address should you assign to the virtual machine?

A. Dynamic IP address

B. Static IP address

C. Private IP address

D. Public IP address

Answer: D. Public IP address

Question 12:

Which Azure component is used to control traffic between different Azure virtual networks?

A. Azure DNS

B. Azure Resource Manager

C. Azure Traffic Manager

D. Azure VNet Peering

Answer: D. Azure VNet Peering

Question 13:

You want to define custom routes to guide traffic within an Azure virtual network. What should you use?

A. Azure VPN Gateway

B. Azure ExpressRoute

C. User-Defined Routes (UDR)

D. Azure Firewall

Answer: C. User-Defined Routes (UDR)

Question 14:

What is the main purpose of Azure Service Endpoints?

A. To establish private connections from a virtual network to Azure services

B. To provide public internet access to Azure services

C. To manage DNS settings for Azure resources

D. To configure firewall rules for Azure services

Answer: A. To establish private connections from a virtual network to Azure services

Question 15:

You want to control inbound and outbound traffic to network resources in Azure by defining rules based on source, destination, and port. What should you use?

A. Azure DNS

B. Network Security Groups (NSGs)

C. Azure Service Endpoints

D. Azure Private Endpoint

Answer: B. Network Security Groups (NSGs)

Question 16:

What is the primary role of Azure Firewall in an Azure virtual network?

A. To manage domain name system (DNS) settings

B. To establish secure connections to Azure services

C. To centralize network security and filtering of traffic

D. To configure custom routes for network traffic

Answer: C. To centralize network security and filtering of traffic

Question 17:

You need to create a secure and private connection between an Azure virtual network and Azure SQL Database. What feature should you use?

A. Azure VPN Gateway

B. Azure ExpressRoute

C. Azure Service Endpoint

D. Azure Private Endpoint

Answer: D. Azure Private Endpoint

Question 18:

What is the primary role of Azure DNS in Azure virtual networking?

A. To create secure connections to Azure services

B. To allocate IP addresses to virtual machines

C. To manage DNS zones and records for Azure resources

D. To define network security group rules

Answer: C. To manage DNS zones and records for Azure resources

Question 19:

You want to allow multiple Azure virtual networks to communicate with each other. What feature should you configure?

A. Azure Traffic Manager

B. Azure VNet Peering

C. Azure ExpressRoute

D. Azure Resource Manager

Answer: B. Azure VNet Peering

Question 20:

What is the primary function of a public IP address in Azure?

A. To identify and locate resources in a virtual network

B. To create network security group rules

C. To configure domain name system (DNS) settings

D. To provide public internet access to Azure resources

Answer: D. To provide public internet access to Azure resources

Question 21:

Which component in Azure allows you to control the flow of traffic between Azure virtual networks?

A. Azure Resource Manager

B. Azure Traffic Manager

C. Azure VNet Peering

D. Azure DNS

Answer: C. Azure VNet Peering

Question 22:

You want to ensure that only a specific set of users can delete Azure resources while others are restricted from deleting resources. What should you use?

A. Azure Policies

B. Role-Based Access Control (RBAC)

C. Resource Locks

D. Custom Tags

Answer: C. Resource Locks

Question 23:

What is the primary purpose of Azure Firewall in Azure networking?

A. To provide domain name system (DNS) services for virtual networks

B. To establish secure, private connections to Azure services

C. To centralize network-level protection and filtering of traffic

D. To configure user-defined routes for network traffic

Answer: C. To centralize network-level protection and filtering of traffic

Question 24:

You need to establish a secure, private connection between an Azure virtual network and Azure SQL Database. What feature should you use?

A. Azure VPN Gateway

B. Azure ExpressRoute

C. Azure Service Endpoint

D. Azure Private Endpoint

Answer: D. Azure Private Endpoint

Question 25:

What is the main purpose of Azure DNS in the Azure environment?

A. To manage domain name system (DNS) settings for virtual networks

B. To allocate IP addresses to Azure resources

C. To establish secure connections to Azure services

D. To configure firewall rules for Azure services

Answer: A. To manage domain name system (DNS) settings for virtual networks

Question 26:

You want to define custom routes to guide traffic within an Azure virtual network. What should you use?

A. Azure VPN Gateway

B. Azure ExpressRoute

C. User-Defined Routes (UDR)

D. Azure Firewall

Answer: C. User-Defined Routes (UDR)

Question 27:

What is the primary function of Azure Service Endpoints?

A. To establish private connections from a virtual network to Azure services

B. To provide public internet access to Azure services

C. To manage DNS settings for Azure resources

D. To allocate IP addresses to virtual machines

Answer: A. To establish private connections from a virtual network to Azure services

Question 28:

You need to control inbound and outbound traffic to network resources in Azure by defining rules based on source, destination, and port. What should you use?

A. Azure DNS

B. Network Security Groups (NSGs)

C. Azure Service Endpoints

D. Azure Private Endpoint

Answer: B. Network Security Groups (NSGs)

Question 29:

What is the primary role of Azure Firewall in an Azure virtual network?

A. To manage domain name system (DNS) settings

B. To establish secure connections to Azure services

C. To centralize network security and filtering of traffic

D. To configure custom routes for network traffic

Answer: C. To centralize network security and filtering of traffic

Question 30:

You want to create a secure and private connection between an Azure virtual network and Azure SQL Database. What feature should you use?

A. Azure VPN Gateway

B. Azure ExpressRoute

C. Azure Service Endpoint

D. Azure Private Endpoint

Answer: D. Azure Private Endpoint

These review questions and answers cover a range of topics related to virtual networking in Azure, helping you prepare for certification exams and deepen your understanding of Azure networking concepts.

Chapter 4: Intersite Connectivity

In the ever-evolving landscape of cloud computing, creating seamless connectivity between different environments is crucial. Azure, Microsoft's cloud platform, provides a plethora of tools and services for establishing connectivity between Azure regions, on-premises data centers, and other cloud platforms. This chapter delves into the intricate world of intersite connectivity within Azure, encompassing Azure-to-Azure connectivity, Azure to on-premises connectivity, intersite connectivity architecture, and the formidable Virtual WAN.

Azure-to-Azure Connectivity: Bridging the Cloud

Azure offers a multitude of services to facilitate connectivity between different Azure regions, enabling organizations to build geographically dispersed yet interconnected cloud environments.

Key Aspects of Azure-to-Azure Connectivity:

Azure Virtual Network Peering: Utilize virtual network peering to establish seamless and secure communication between virtual networks in different Azure regions.

Global VNet Peering: Extend peering capabilities globally, providing connectivity across Azure regions worldwide.

Azure ExpressRoute: Employ Azure ExpressRoute to establish private, dedicated connections to Azure data centers from different regions.

Azure to On-Premises Connectivity: Bridging the Physical and Digital Worlds

Organizations often require connectivity between their on-premises data centers and Azure for hybrid cloud scenarios. Azure offers various solutions to bridge these two worlds effectively.

Azure to On-Premises Connectivity Solutions: Azure Site-to-Site VPN: Set up site-to-site VPN connections to securely connect on-premises networks to Azure VNets.

Azure ExpressRoute: Leverage Azure ExpressRoute for dedicated and high-bandwidth connections between on-premises and Azure data centers.

Azure VPN Gateway: Deploy Azure VPN Gateways to establish point-to-site VPN connections for remote users or branch offices.

Intersite Connectivity Architecture: A Holistic Approach

A well-architected intersite connectivity solution considers a variety of components, including Azure VNets, on-premises networks, security, and performance. Designing a robust architecture is pivotal to achieving seamless and efficient communication.

Intersite Connectivity Architecture Essentials:

Network Planning: Careful planning is essential for defining address spaces, routing, and addressing security requirements.

Security Considerations: Implement security measures, such as Network Security Groups (NSGs), to protect data in transit between sites.

Performance Optimization: Optimize network performance by selecting the appropriate connectivity methods and services.

Virtual WAN: Simplifying Intersite Connectivity

Managing complex intersite connectivity can be challenging, especially for large enterprises. Azure's Virtual WAN is designed to simplify and streamline this process.

Key Components of Azure Virtual WAN:

Hub-and-Spoke Architecture: Virtual WAN employs a hub-and-spoke model, centralizing connectivity through hubs while maintaining isolation between spokes.

Site-to-Site Connectivity: Virtual WAN integrates seamlessly with Azure Site-to-Site VPN and ExpressRoute for connecting branch offices and on-premises data centers.

Global Reach: Extend your network globally with Azure Virtual WAN, allowing for worldwide connectivity.

Security Integration: Enhance security through Azure Firewall and Azure Bastion, integrated with Virtual WAN for threat protection and secure access.

Traffic Optimization: Leverage Azure Virtual WAN's traffic optimization capabilities to ensure efficient data flow.

Intersite connectivity is a fundamental pillar of modern cloud computing, and Azure provides a wealth of tools and services to enable organizations to establish robust and secure connections between different environments. Whether it's Azure-to-Azure connectivity, connectivity between Azure and on-premises data centers, a well-architected intersite connectivity framework, or the simplicity of Azure Virtual WAN, organizations have a rich toolkit at their disposal. By understanding and effectively implementing these solutions, organizations can build interconnected, efficient, and secure cloud environments that support their digital transformation and business objectives.

Exam Essentials for Intersite Connectivity

As you prepare for Microsoft Azure certification exams, including the Microsoft Certified: Azure Administrator Associate (AZ-104) or those focused on intersite connectivity, it's essential to master the key concepts and best practices related to connecting different environments seamlessly within Azure. These exam essentials will help you demonstrate your expertise in establishing connectivity between Azure regions, on-premises data centers, and other cloud platforms.

1. Azure-to-Azure Connectivity

Azure Virtual Network Peering: Understand how to use Azure Virtual Network peering to connect virtual networks within different Azure regions.

Global VNet Peering: Learn to extend virtual network peering globally to facilitate connectivity across Azure regions worldwide.

Azure ExpressRoute: Grasp the significance of Azure ExpressRoute in creating private, dedicated connections between Azure data centers in various regions.

2. Azure to On-Premises Connectivity

Azure Site-to-Site VPN: Master the setup and configuration of Azure Site-to-Site VPN connections, enabling secure communication between on-premises networks and Azure VNets.

Azure ExpressRoute: Understand the role of Azure ExpressRoute in providing high-bandwidth, dedicated connections between on-premises data centers and Azure.

Azure VPN Gateway: Learn to deploy Azure VPN Gateways to establish point-to-site VPN connections for remote users and branch offices.

3. Intersite Connectivity Architecture

Network Planning: Recognize the importance of careful planning, including defining address spaces, routing, and addressing security requirements, to design a robust intersite connectivity architecture.

Security Considerations: Implement security measures, such as Network Security Groups (NSGs), to protect data in transit between sites and ensure compliance with security policies.

Performance Optimization: Optimize network performance by selecting the appropriate connectivity methods and services to meet the organization's requirements.

4. Virtual WAN

Hub-and-Spoke Architecture: Understand how Azure Virtual WAN employs a hub-and-spoke model, centralizing connectivity through hubs while maintaining isolation between spokes for efficient network management.

Site-to-Site Connectivity: Leverage Azure Virtual WAN to integrate with Azure Site-to-Site VPN and ExpressRoute, facilitating connectivity between branch offices and on-premises data centers.

Global Reach: Recognize the ability of Azure Virtual WAN to extend the network globally, providing worldwide connectivity for organizations with a global presence.

Security Integration: Learn about security features integrated with Azure Virtual WAN, including Azure Firewall and Azure Bastion, for enhanced threat protection and secure access.

Traffic Optimization: Utilize Azure Virtual WAN's traffic optimization capabilities to ensure efficient data flow across interconnected sites.

By focusing on these exam essentials for intersite connectivity, you'll be well-prepared to excel in this domain during your certification exam. Practical experience, hands-on labs, and real-world practice with Azure networking tools are equally crucial in reinforcing your knowledge and skills. These essentials will not only aid in exam success but also prove invaluable in effectively designing and managing intersite connectivity solutions in Azure to support your organization's digital transformation goals.

Review Questions and Answers

Question 1:

You need to establish a secure connection between an Azure virtual network and your on-premises data center. Which Azure service should you use?

A. Azure Virtual WAN

B. Azure Site-to-Site VPN

C. Azure ExpressRoute

D. Azure VPN Gateway

Answer: C. Azure ExpressRoute

Question 2:

What is the primary purpose of Azure Virtual WAN's hub-and-spoke architecture?

A. To centralize network security

B. To create high-availability connections

C. To simplify network management

D. To increase network bandwidth

Answer: C. To simplify network management

Question 3:

You want to ensure that only a specific set of users can modify Azure resources while others have read-only access. Which built-in Role-Based Access Control (RBAC) role should you assign?

A. Contributor

B. Owner

C. Reader

D. Network Contributor

Answer: A. Contributor

Question 4:

What does the Azure Site-to-Site VPN service facilitate?

A. Secure connections between Azure VNets

B. High-bandwidth dedicated connections to Azure

C. Point-to-site VPN connections for remote users

D. Connectivity between on-premises networks and Azure VNets

Answer: D. Connectivity between on-premises networks and Azure VNets

Question 5:

Which Azure service allows you to configure and manage private, dedicated connections to Azure data centers from your on-premises network?

A. Azure VPN Gateway

B. Azure ExpressRoute

C. Azure Virtual WAN

D. Azure Site-to-Site VPN

Answer: B. Azure ExpressRoute

Question 6:

You need to establish point-to-site VPN connections for remote users or branch offices. What Azure service should you use?

A. Azure Virtual WAN

B. Azure ExpressRoute

C. Azure Site-to-Site VPN

D. Azure VPN Gateway

Answer: D. Azure VPN Gateway

Question 7:

What is the primary purpose of the hub in Azure Virtual WAN's hub-and-spoke architecture?

A. To increase network bandwidth

B. To centralize network security

C. To simplify network management

D. To provide high-availability connections

Answer: C. To centralize network security

Question 8:

Which Azure Virtual WAN feature facilitates secure access to Azure resources from remote locations?

A. Azure VPN Gateway

B. Azure Firewall

C. Azure Bastion

D. Network Security Groups (NSGs)

Answer: C. Azure Bastion

Question 9:

You need to extend your network's reach to global locations and maintain worldwide connectivity. Which Azure service should you use?

A. Azure VPN Gateway

B. Azure Virtual WAN

C. Azure ExpressRoute

D. Azure Site-to-Site VPN

Answer: B. Azure Virtual WAN

Question 10:

What is the primary purpose of Azure Virtual WAN's traffic optimization capabilities?

A. To enhance security

B. To centralize network management

C. To ensure efficient data flow

D. To increase network bandwidth

Answer: C. To ensure efficient data flow

Question 11:

You want to allow multiple Azure virtual networks to communicate with each other. What Azure feature should you configure?

A. Azure Virtual WAN

B. Azure Virtual Network Peering

C. Azure Site-to-Site VPN

D. Azure ExpressRoute

Answer: B. Azure Virtual Network Peering

Question 12:

What does Azure ExpressRoute provide for connecting on-premises data centers to Azure?

A. High-bandwidth connections

B. Point-to-site VPNs

C. Public internet access

D. Secure network security

Answer: A. High-bandwidth connections

Question 13:

You need to extend virtual network peering capabilities globally. What should you use to achieve this in Azure?

A. Azure Virtual Network Peering

B. Azure Site-to-Site VPN

C. Global VNet Peering

D. Azure ExpressRoute

Answer: C. Global VNet Peering

Question 14:

What is the primary function of an Azure Virtual Network Peering connection?

A. To establish secure connections to Azure services

B. To connect on-premises data centers to Azure

C. To facilitate secure communication between virtual networks

D. To centralize network security and filtering of traffic

Answer: C. To facilitate secure communication between virtual networks

Question 15:

You need to allow users to view resources within an Azure resource group but not make any changes. Which built-in Role-Based Access Control (RBAC) role should you assign?

A. Contributor

B. Owner

C. Reader

D. User

Answer: C. Reader

Question 16:

What is the primary role of Azure Firewall within Azure Virtual WAN?

A. To provide domain name system (DNS) services

B. To centralize network management

C. To establish secure connections to Azure services

D. To protect against threats and filter network traffic

Answer: D. To protect against threats and filter network traffic

Question 17:

You need to create a private, dedicated connection between your on-premises data center and Azure. Which Azure service should you use?

A. Azure VPN Gateway

B. Azure Site-to-Site VPN

C. Azure Virtual WAN

D. Azure ExpressRoute

Answer: D. Azure ExpressRoute

Question 18:

What is the purpose of a point-to-site VPN connection in Azure?

A. To connect on-premises data centers to Azure VNets

B. To establish secure connections to Azure services

C. To allow remote users or branch offices to connect to Azure resources

D. To centralize network security in Azure Virtual WAN

Answer: C. To allow remote users or branch offices to connect to Azure resources

Question 19:

You want to centralize network security and efficiently manage connectivity in Azure Virtual WAN. What architecture model does Azure Virtual WAN employ?

A. Mesh architecture

B. Hub-and-spoke architecture

C. Star topology

D. Ring topology

Answer: B. Hub-and-spoke architecture

Question 20:

What is the primary purpose of the spoke in Azure Virtual WAN's hub-and-spoke architecture?

A. To centralize network security

B. To simplify network management

C. To provide high-availability connections

D. To increase network bandwidth

Answer: B. To simplify network management

Question 21:

You need to configure a secure, private connection between Azure virtual networks in different Azure regions. What should you use?

A. Azure Virtual Network Peering

B. Azure Virtual WAN

C. Azure Site-to-Site VPN

D. Azure ExpressRoute

Answer: A. Azure Virtual Network Peering

Question 22:

What role is played by the hub in Azure Virtual WAN's hub-and-spoke architecture?

A. To centralize network security

B. To simplify network management

C. To provide high-availability connections

D. To increase network bandwidth

Answer: A. To centralize network security

Question 23:

What is the primary function of Azure Virtual WAN's traffic optimization capabilities?

A. To enhance security

B. To centralize network management

C. To ensure efficient data flow

D. To increase network bandwidth

Answer: C. To ensure efficient data flow

Question 24:

You want to ensure that only a specific set of users can modify Azure resources while others have read-only access. Which built-in Role-Based Access Control (RBAC) role should you assign?

A. Contributor

B. Owner

C. Reader

D. Network Contributor

Answer: A. Contributor

Question 25:

Which Azure service allows you to configure and manage private, dedicated connections to Azure data centers from your on-premises network?

A. Azure VPN Gateway

B. Azure Site-to-Site VPN

C. Azure ExpressRoute

D. Azure Virtual WAN

Answer: C. Azure ExpressRoute

Question 26:

You need to establish point-to-site VPN connections for remote users or branch offices. What Azure service should you use?

A. Azure Virtual WAN

B. Azure ExpressRoute

C. Azure Site-to-Site VPN

D. Azure VPN Gateway

Answer: D. Azure VPN Gateway

Question 27:

What is the primary purpose of the hub in Azure Virtual WAN's hub-and-spoke architecture?

A. To increase network bandwidth

B. To centralize network security

C. To simplify network management

D. To provide high-availability connections

Answer: B. To centralize network security

Question 28:

Which Azure Virtual WAN feature facilitates secure access to Azure resources from remote locations?

A. Azure VPN Gateway

B. Azure Firewall

C. Azure Bastion

D. Network Security Groups (NSGs)

Answer: C. Azure Bastion

Question 29:

You need to extend your network's reach to global locations and maintain worldwide connectivity. Which Azure service should you use?

A. Azure VPN Gateway

B. Azure Virtual WAN

C. Azure ExpressRoute

D. Azure Site-to-Site VPN

Answer: B. Azure Virtual WAN

Question 30:

What is the primary purpose of Azure Virtual WAN's traffic optimization capabilities?

A. To enhance security

B. To centralize network management

C. To ensure efficient data flow

D. To increase network bandwidth

Answer: C. To ensure efficient data flow

Question 31:

You want to allow users to view resources within an Azure resource group but not make any changes. Which built-in Role-Based Access Control (RBAC) role should you assign?

A. Contributor

B. Owner

C. Reader

D. User

Answer: C. Reader

Question 32:

What is the primary role of Azure Firewall within Azure Virtual WAN?

A. To provide domain name system (DNS) services

B. To centralize network management

C. To establish secure connections to Azure services

D. To protect against threats and filter network traffic

Answer: D. To protect against threats and filter network traffic

Question 33:

You need to create a private, dedicated connection between your on-premises data center and Azure. Which Azure service should you use?

A. Azure VPN Gateway

B. Azure Site-to-Site VPN

C. Azure Virtual WAN

D. Azure ExpressRoute

Answer: D. Azure ExpressRoute

Question 34:

What is the purpose of a point-to-site VPN connection in Azure?

A. To connect on-premises data centers to Azure VNets

B. To establish secure connections to Azure services

C. To allow remote users or branch offices to connect to Azure resources

D. To centralize network security in Azure Virtual WAN

Answer: C. To allow remote users or branch offices to connect to Azure resources

Question 35:

You want to centralize network security and efficiently manage connectivity in Azure Virtual WAN. What architecture model does Azure Virtual WAN employ?

A. Mesh architecture

B. Hub-and-spoke architecture

C. Star topology

D. Ring topology

Answer: B. Hub-and-spoke architecture

Question 36:

What is the primary purpose of the spoke in Azure Virtual WAN's hub-and-spoke architecture?

A. To centralize network security

B. To simplify network management

C. To provide high-availability connections

D. To increase network bandwidth

Answer: B. To simplify network management

Question 37:

You need to configure a secure, private connection between Azure virtual networks in different Azure regions. What should you use?

A. Azure Virtual Network Peering

B. Azure Virtual WAN

C. Azure Site-to-Site VPN

D. Azure ExpressRoute

Answer: A. Azure Virtual Network Peering

Question 38:

What role is played by the hub in Azure Virtual WAN's hub-and-spoke architecture?

A. To centralize network security

B. To simplify network management

C. To provide high-availability connections

D. To increase network bandwidth

Answer: A. To centralize network security

Question 39:

What is the primary function of Azure Virtual WAN's traffic optimization capabilities?

A. To enhance security

B. To centralize network management

C. To ensure efficient data flow

D. To increase network bandwidth

Answer: C. To ensure efficient data flow

Question 40:

You want to allow users to view resources within an Azure resource group but not make any changes. Which built-in Role-Based Access Control (RBAC) role should you assign?

A. Contributor

B. Owner

C. Reader

D. User

Answer: C. Reader

Chapter 5: Network Traffic Management

In the dynamic world of cloud computing, ensuring the availability, performance, and security of applications and services is of paramount importance. Network traffic management is the cornerstone that supports these objectives. Microsoft Azure, a leading cloud platform, offers a suite of tools and services designed to effectively manage network traffic and ensure that applications and services are accessible, responsive, and secure. In this chapter, we explore the various aspects of network traffic management within Azure, including availability options, Azure Load Balancer, Azure Application Gateway, Azure Front Door, Azure Traffic Manager, and a comparison of these load balancing solutions.

Availability Options: Ensuring Uptime

Ensuring high availability is a top priority for any organization, and Azure provides several options to achieve this goal. These options include fault tolerance, redundancy, and geographic distribution.

Key Availability Options in Azure:

Availability Zones: Azure Availability Zones are physically separate data centers within an Azure region, providing fault tolerance and high availability for mission-critical applications.

Availability Sets: Create availability sets to distribute virtual machines across different fault domains and update domains, reducing the risk of downtime during maintenance.

Geo-Replication: Azure offers geo-replication for data, databases, and services, enabling data redundancy and recovery in different geographic regions.

Azure Load Balancer: Distributing Traffic

Azure Load Balancer is a crucial component for evenly distributing network traffic to multiple virtual machines, enhancing application availability and fault tolerance.

Azure Load Balancer Essentials:

Load Balancing Algorithms: Understand load balancing algorithms like Round Robin and Least Connections to determine how traffic is distributed.

Back-End Pools: Configure back-end pools to define the virtual machines that will receive load-balanced traffic.

Health Probes: Set up health probes to monitor the status of virtual machines and automatically route traffic away from unhealthy instances.

Azure Application Gateway: Optimizing Web Applications

Azure Application Gateway is a layer 7 load balancer designed to optimize the performance and security of web applications.

Key Aspects of Azure Application Gateway:

Web Application Firewall (WAF): Enable the WAF on Azure Application Gateway to protect web applications from common web vulnerabilities and attacks.

Routing Rules: Configure routing rules to manage traffic distribution, routing requests to different back-end pools based on URL paths or host headers.

Session Affinity: Implement session affinity to ensure that client requests are consistently routed to the same back-end instance.

Azure Front Door: Global Content Delivery

Azure Front Door is a global content delivery network (CDN) service that optimizes web applications for fast and secure global access.

Azure Front Door Features:

Global Load Balancing: Use Azure Front Door's global load balancing capabilities to direct traffic to the closest and most available instance for reduced latency.

Web Application Acceleration: Accelerate web applications and content delivery to enhance user experiences.

Security and DDoS Protection: Implement security features, including Web Application Firewall (WAF) and DDoS protection, to safeguard applications from threats.

Azure Traffic Manager: DNS-Based Traffic Routing

Azure Traffic Manager is a DNS-based traffic routing service that directs client requests to the most suitable service endpoint based on configured routing methods.

Key Features of Azure Traffic Manager:

Traffic Routing Methods: Explore traffic routing methods such as Priority, Weighted, Geographic, and Performance-based routing to achieve specific objectives.

Endpoint Monitoring: Configure endpoint monitoring to ensure the health and availability of service endpoints.

Geographic Traffic Distribution: Use geographic routing to route traffic to specific endpoints based on the geographic location of clients.

Comparing the Load Balancing Solutions

To make informed decisions about network traffic management in Azure, it's essential to compare the available load balancing solutions, considering factors like use cases, capabilities, and limitations.

Comparison of Load Balancing Solutions:

Azure Load Balancer vs. Azure Application Gateway: Differentiate between the scenarios where Azure Load Balancer and Azure Application Gateway are best suited, based on their load balancing capabilities and features.

Azure Application Gateway vs. Azure Front Door: Understand the distinctions between Azure Application Gateway and Azure Front Door in terms of content optimization, security, and global delivery.

Azure Front Door vs. Azure Traffic Manager: Compare Azure Front Door and Azure Traffic Manager, considering their respective roles in optimizing content delivery and routing traffic.

Load Balancing Decision Factors: Consider factors such as application type, load balancing requirements, security needs, and geographic distribution when choosing the most suitable load balancing solution.

Network traffic management is a critical component of cloud infrastructure, and Azure provides a rich set of tools and services to address the diverse needs of organizations. Whether it's achieving high availability through availability options, load balancing with Azure Load Balancer, optimizing web applications using Azure Application Gateway, global content delivery via Azure Front Door, or DNS-based traffic routing with Azure Traffic Manager, Azure's network traffic management solutions empower organizations to deliver applications and services with the utmost reliability, performance, and security. Understanding the intricacies of these solutions is essential for cloud administrators and architects to make informed decisions and design robust network architectures that meet their organization's objectives.

Exam Essentials for Network Traffic Management

As you prepare for Microsoft Azure certification exams, including the Microsoft Certified: Azure Administrator Associate (AZ-104) or those focused on network traffic management, it's essential to master the key concepts and best practices related to efficiently managing network traffic within the Azure environment. These exam essentials will help you demonstrate your expertise in optimizing application availability, load balancing, and content delivery.

1. Availability Options

Azure Availability Zones: Understand the concept of Availability Zones, which provide physical data center redundancy within Azure regions to ensure high availability.

Availability Sets: Learn how to create and configure Availability Sets to distribute virtual machines across fault domains and update domains for fault tolerance.

Geo-Replication: Grasp the importance of geo-replication for data, databases, and services, allowing data redundancy and disaster recovery in different geographic regions.

2. Azure Load Balancer

Load Balancing Algorithms: Familiarize yourself with load balancing algorithms like Round Robin and Least Connections to control how traffic is distributed among back-end resources.

Back-End Pools: Learn to configure back-end pools to specify the virtual machines that will receive load-balanced traffic.

Health Probes: Understand the role of health probes in monitoring the status of back-end resources and automatically routing traffic away from unhealthy instances.

3. Azure Application Gateway

Web Application Firewall (WAF): Explore the functionalities of the Web Application Firewall (WAF) integrated with Azure Application Gateway to protect web applications from common vulnerabilities and attacks.

Routing Rules: Master the configuration of routing rules to manage traffic distribution based on URL paths or host headers, routing requests to different back-end pools.

Session Affinity: Learn how to implement session affinity to ensure that client requests are consistently directed to the same back-end resource, which can be crucial for maintaining application state.

4. Azure Front Door

Global Load Balancing: Understand how Azure Front Door uses global load balancing to route traffic to the closest and most available instance, reducing latency for global users.

Web Application Acceleration: Grasp the capabilities of Azure Front Door in accelerating web applications and content delivery, enhancing user experiences.

Security and DDoS Protection: Explore the security features offered by Azure Front Door, including Web Application Firewall (WAF) and protection against Distributed Denial of Service (DDoS) attacks.

5. Azure Traffic Manager

Traffic Routing Methods: Familiarize yourself with various traffic routing methods, including Priority, Weighted, Geographic, and Performance-based routing, to determine the most suitable routing method for specific scenarios.

Endpoint Monitoring: Learn how to configure endpoint monitoring to ensure the health and availability of service endpoints.

Geographic Traffic Distribution: Understand the use of geographic routing in Azure Traffic Manager to route traffic to specific endpoints based on the geographic location of clients.

6. Comparing the Load Balancing Solutions

Use Cases and Scenarios: Be able to distinguish between Azure Load Balancer, Azure Application Gateway, Azure Front Door, and Azure Traffic Manager based on use cases, load balancing capabilities, and limitations.

Selection Criteria: Consider various factors such as application type, load balancing requirements, security needs, and geographic distribution when deciding which load balancing solution to use.

Integration and Coexistence: Understand how these load balancing solutions can integrate or coexist in a single architecture to provide comprehensive traffic management.

By focusing on these exam essentials for network traffic management in Azure, you will be well-prepared to excel in this domain during your certification exam. Practical experience, hands-on labs, and real-world practice with Azure networking tools are equally crucial in reinforcing your knowledge and skills. These essentials will not only aid in exam success but also prove invaluable in effectively designing and managing network traffic management solutions in the Azure cloud environment.

Review Questions And Answers

Question 1:

What is the primary purpose of Azure Availability Zones?

A. To optimize traffic routing

B. To provide data center redundancy within a region

C. To distribute load-balanced traffic

D. To route traffic to the closest instance

Answer: B. To provide data center redundancy within a region

Question 2:

Which Azure service is used to distribute network traffic across multiple virtual machines to enhance application availability?

A. Azure ExpressRoute

B. Azure Traffic Manager

C. Azure Load Balancer

D. Azure Application Gateway

Answer: C. Azure Load Balancer

Question 3:

What is the role of health probes in Azure Load Balancer?

A. To protect against DDoS attacks

B. To configure routing rules

C. To monitor the status of back-end resources

D. To accelerate web applications

Answer: C. To monitor the status of back-end resources

Question 4:

Azure Application Gateway is primarily designed for optimizing the performance and security of:

A. Virtual machines

B. Web applications

C. Databases

D. IoT devices

Answer: B. Web applications

Question 5:

What is the purpose of the Web Application Firewall (WAF) in Azure Application Gateway?

A. To protect against DDoS attacks

B. To optimize web application performance

C. To enhance database security

D. To safeguard web applications from common web vulnerabilities and attacks

Answer: D. To safeguard web applications from common web vulnerabilities and attacks

Question 6:

Which Azure service is a global content delivery network (CDN) that optimizes web applications for fast and secure global access?

A. Azure Load Balancer

B. Azure Application Gateway

C. Azure Front Door

D. Azure Traffic Manager

Answer: C. Azure Front Door

Question 7:

Azure Front Door employs global load balancing to:

A. Accelerate web applications

B. Route traffic to the closest and most available instance

C. Optimize traffic routing

D. Provide data center redundancy

Answer: B. Route traffic to the closest and most available instance

Question 8:

What security feature is integrated with Azure Front Door to protect web applications from common web vulnerabilities and attacks?

A. DDoS Protection

B. Load Balancer

C. Web Application Firewall (WAF)

D. Traffic Manager

Answer: C. Web Application Firewall (WAF)

Question 9:

Azure Traffic Manager is a DNS-based traffic routing service that directs client requests to the most suitable service endpoint based on:

A. Priority and Weighted routing

B. Geographic location of clients

C. URL paths and host headers

D. Load balancing algorithms

Answer: B. Geographic location of clients

Question 10:

What is the primary function of traffic routing methods in Azure Traffic Manager?

A. To monitor endpoint health

B. To configure back-end pools

C. To route traffic based on geographic location

D. To determine how client requests are directed to endpoints

Answer: D. To determine how client requests are directed to endpoints

Question 11:

Which Azure service is designed to route traffic based on URL paths and host headers, allowing requests to be directed to different back-end pools?

A. Azure Application Gateway

B. Azure Front Door

C. Azure Load Balancer

D. Azure Traffic Manager

Answer: A. Azure Application Gateway

Question 12:

Azure Load Balancer primarily operates at which layer of the OSI model?

A. Layer 2 (Data Link Layer)

B. Layer 3 (Network Layer)

C. Layer 4 (Transport Layer)

D. Layer 7 (Application Layer)

Answer: B. Layer 3 (Network Layer)

Question 13:

What is the main purpose of Azure Traffic Manager?

A. Load balancing

B. Web application optimization

C. DNS-based traffic routing

D. Data center redundancy

Answer: C. DNS-based traffic routing

Question 14:

In Azure, what is the role of Availability Sets?

A. To optimize traffic routing

B. To create fault tolerance

C. To distribute load-balanced traffic

D. To configure routing rules

Answer: B. To create fault tolerance

Question 15:

Which Azure service uses geo-replication to provide data redundancy and recovery in different geographic regions?

A. Azure Traffic Manager

B. Azure Front Door

C. Azure Load Balancer

D. Azure Availability Zones

Answer: D. Azure Availability Zones

Question 16:

What load balancing algorithm distributes traffic to the next available instance in a circular manner?

A. Round Robin

B. Least Connections

C. Priority-based routing

D. Geographic routing

Answer: A. Round Robin

Question 17:

Azure Front Door accelerates web applications and content delivery by reducing:

A. Security risks

B. Latency for global users

C. Load balancing complexity

D. Data center redundancy

Answer: B. Latency for global users

Question 18:

What is the primary role of the Web Application Firewall (WAF) in Azure Front Door?

A. To protect against DDoS attacks

B. To optimize web application performance

C. To enhance database security

D. To safeguard web applications from common web vulnerabilities and attacks

Answer: D. To safeguard web applications from common web vulnerabilities and attacks

Question 19:

In Azure Traffic Manager, what is the primary purpose of Priority-based routing?

A. To monitor endpoint health

B. To configure back-end pools

C. To route traffic based on geographic location

D. To give precedence to specific endpoints

Answer: D. To give precedence to specific endpoints

Question 20:

Which Azure service allows traffic to be distributed based on the geographic location of clients?

A. Azure Application Gateway

B. Azure Front Door

C. Azure Load Balancer

D. Azure Traffic Manager

Answer: D. Azure Traffic Manager

Question 21:

Azure Load Balancer operates at which layer of the OSI model to distribute network traffic?

A. Layer 2 (Data Link Layer)

B. Layer 3 (Network Layer)

C. Layer 4 (Transport Layer)

D. Layer 7 (Application Layer)

Answer: B. Layer 3 (Network Layer)

Question 22:

What feature of Azure Application Gateway enables traffic distribution based on URL paths and host headers?

A. Back-End Pools

B. Health Probes

C. Session Affinity

D. Routing Rules

Answer: D. Routing Rules

Question 23:

Azure Front Door primarily uses what mechanism to reduce latency and optimize web application performance?

A. Content delivery network (CDN)

B. Load balancing algorithms

C. Session affinity

D. Round Robin

Answer: A. Content delivery network (CDN)

Question 24:

What is the primary purpose of the Priority traffic routing method in Azure Traffic Manager?

A. To monitor endpoint health

B. To configure back-end pools

C. To route traffic based on geographic location

D. To give precedence to specific endpoints

Answer: D. To give precedence to specific endpoints

Question 25:

Which Azure service is best suited for routing client requests to the closest and most available instance?

A. Azure Application Gateway

B. Azure Front Door

C. Azure Load Balancer

D. Azure Traffic Manager

Answer: B. Azure Front Door

Question 26:

What is the role of health probes in Azure Application Gateway?

A. To protect against DDoS attacks

B. To configure routing rules

C. To monitor the status of back-end resources

D. To accelerate web applications

Answer: C. To monitor the status of back-end resources

Question 27:

Which Azure service provides global load balancing for traffic routing?

A. Azure Load Balancer

B. Azure Application Gateway

C. Azure Front Door

D. Azure Traffic Manager

Answer: C. Azure Front Door

Question 28:

What security feature is integrated with Azure Application Gateway to protect web applications from common web vulnerabilities and attacks?

A. DDoS Protection

B. Load Balancer

C. Web Application Firewall (WAF)

D. Traffic Manager

Answer: C. Web Application Firewall (WAF)

Question 29:

Azure Traffic Manager primarily operates at which layer of the OSI model to route traffic based on DNS?

A. Layer 2 (Data Link Layer)

B. Layer 3 (Network Layer)

C. Layer 4 (Transport Layer)

D. Layer 7 (Application Layer)

Answer: D. Layer 7 (Application Layer)

Question 30:

What is the main purpose of the Weighted traffic routing method in Azure Traffic Manager?

A. To monitor endpoint health

B. To configure back-end pools

C. To route traffic based on geographic location

D. To distribute traffic based on a weight assigned to each endpoint

Answer: D. To distribute traffic based on a weight assigned to each endpoint

Question 31:

In Azure Load Balancer, which load balancing algorithm distributes traffic to the instance with the fewest active connections?

A. Round Robin

B. Least Connections

C. Priority-based routing

D. Geographic routing

Answer: B. Least Connections

Question 32:

What is the primary role of Traffic Manager in Azure?

A. To load balance traffic

B. To optimize web applications

C. To route traffic based on DNS

D. To provide data center redundancy

Answer: C. To route traffic based on DNS

Question 33:

Which Azure service is designed to accelerate web applications and content delivery for global users?

A. Azure Load Balancer

B. Azure Application Gateway

C. Azure Front Door

D. Azure Traffic Manager

Answer: C. Azure Front Door

Question 34:

In Azure Traffic Manager, what is the primary purpose of Geographic traffic routing?

A. To monitor endpoint health

B. To configure back-end pools

C. To route traffic based on geographic location

D. To distribute traffic based on a weight assigned to each endpoint

Answer: C. To route traffic based on geographic location

Question 35:

What is the primary purpose of Geographic traffic routing in Azure Traffic Manager?

A. To monitor endpoint health

B. To configure back-end pools

C. To route traffic based on geographic location

D. To optimize web application performance

Answer: C. To route traffic based on geographic location

Question 36:

Which Azure service is designed to optimize the performance and security of web applications?

A. Azure ExpressRoute

B. Azure Traffic Manager

C. Azure Load Balancer

D. Azure Application Gateway

Answer: D. Azure Application Gateway

Question 37:

Azure Front Door is a global content delivery network (CDN) service designed to:

A. Route traffic based on DNS

B. Optimize web applications for fast and secure global access

C. Protect against DDoS attacks

D. Distribute traffic among virtual machines

Answer: B. Optimize web applications for fast and secure global access

Question 38:

Which traffic routing method in Azure Traffic Manager is designed to direct client requests to specific endpoints based on their priority?

A. Round Robin

B. Weighted

C. Priority

D. Geographic

Answer: C. Priority

Question 39:

What is the primary function of Weighted traffic routing in Azure Traffic Manager?

A. To monitor endpoint health

B. To configure back-end pools

C. To route traffic based on geographic location

D. To distribute traffic based on a weight assigned to each endpoint

Answer: D. To distribute traffic based on a weight assigned to each endpoint

Question 40:

Which Azure service provides a layer 7 load balancer designed to optimize the performance and security of web applications?

A. Azure Load Balancer

B. Azure Application Gateway

C. Azure Front Door

D. Azure Traffic Manager

Answer: B. Azure Application Gateway

Question 41:

In Azure Load Balancer, what is the primary role of Back-End Pools?

A. To protect against DDoS attacks

B. To configure routing rules

C. To monitor the status of back-end resources

D. To define the virtual machines that will receive load-balanced traffic

Answer: D. To define the virtual machines that will receive load-balanced traffic

Question 42:

What is the primary purpose of Session Affinity in Azure Application Gateway?

A. To protect against DDoS attacks

B. To optimize web application performance

C. To enhance database security

D. To ensure that client requests are consistently routed to the same back-end instance

Answer: D. To ensure that client requests are consistently routed to the same back-end instance

Question 43:

What is the primary function of Priority-based routing in Azure Traffic Manager?

A. To monitor endpoint health

B. To configure back-end pools

C. To route traffic based on geographic location

D. To give precedence to specific endpoints

Answer: D. To give precedence to specific endpoints

Question 44:

Azure Load Balancer is primarily designed to distribute network traffic at which layer of the OSI model?

A. Layer 2 (Data Link Layer)

B. Layer 3 (Network Layer)

C. Layer 4 (Transport Layer)

D. Layer 7 (Application Layer)

Answer: B. Layer 3 (Network Layer)

Question 45:

Which Azure service is designed to optimize the performance and security of web applications?

A. Azure ExpressRoute

B. Azure Traffic Manager

C. Azure Load Balancer

D. Azure Application Gateway

Answer: D. Azure Application Gateway

Question 46:

Azure Front Door primarily employs what mechanism to reduce latency and optimize web application performance?

A. Content delivery network (CDN)

B. Load balancing algorithms

C. Session affinity

D. Round Robin

Answer: A. Content delivery network (CDN)

Chapter 6: Azure Storage

In the world of cloud computing, data storage is a fundamental building block that underpins the functionality and capabilities of cloud services. Microsoft Azure, a leading cloud platform, offers a robust and versatile Azure Storage system, providing a range of storage services to meet the diverse needs of organizations. This chapter delves into the intricate world of Azure Storage, including Azure Storage Accounts, the various storage services, replication options, storage account types, storage endpoints, Azure Blob Storage, security considerations, Azure Files and File Sync, and the management of Azure Storage resources.

Azure Storage Account: The Gateway to Data Storage

At the heart of Azure Storage is the Azure Storage Account. It serves as the gateway to access and manage various storage services and plays a pivotal role in controlling data availability, durability, and access.

Key Aspects of Azure Storage Accounts:

Storage Account Types: Understand the different types of storage accounts, including General Purpose v2, General Purpose v1, Blob Storage, and Premium, and their respective use cases.

Replication Options: Learn about storage replication options, such as locally redundant storage (LRS), geo-redundant storage (GRS), zone-redundant storage (ZRS), and read-access geo-redundant storage (RA-GRS), for data redundancy and availability.

Access Control: Configure access control and permissions for storage accounts, ensuring data security and compliance.

Azure Storage Services: A Multifaceted Toolbox

Azure Storage offers a range of services, each designed for specific use cases. Understanding the array of services available is crucial for selecting the right one for your storage needs.

Key Azure Storage Services:

Azure Blob Storage: Dive into Azure Blob Storage, designed for unstructured object data, and grasp the concepts of containers and blobs.

Azure Table Storage: Explore Azure Table Storage for semi-structured data storage, providing a NoSQL data store for applications.

Azure Queue Storage: Learn how Azure Queue Storage facilitates messaging between application components and supports asynchronous communication.

Azure File Storage: Understand Azure File Storage for file-based sharing and the management of file shares accessible from multiple virtual machines.

Storage Replication: Data Redundancy and Availability

Data is a critical asset, and Azure offers various replication options to ensure data redundancy and availability in the face of failures or disasters.

Replication Options:

Locally Redundant Storage (LRS): Comprehend LRS, which replicates data within a storage scale unit for high availability.

Geo-Redundant Storage (GRS): Understand GRS, which replicates data to a secondary Azure region for data recovery in case of regional failures.

Zone-Redundant Storage (ZRS): Learn about ZRS, which replicates data across availability zones within a region to ensure high availability.

Read-Access Geo-Redundant Storage (RA-GRS): Grasp RA-GRS, which extends GRS by providing read access to the secondary region for data access and analytics.

Storage Account Types: Tailored for Different Needs

Azure Storage offers a range of storage account types, each optimized for specific workloads and performance requirements.

Storage Account Types:

General Purpose v2 (GPv2): Discover the capabilities of GPv2 accounts, which offer a balance of capacity, transaction rates, and pricing.

General Purpose v1 (GPv1): Understand GPv1 accounts, the earlier version of general-purpose accounts, suited for basic storage needs.

Blob Storage: Explore Blob Storage accounts, ideal for storing unstructured data, such as documents, images, and media files.

Premium: Learn about Premium storage accounts, designed for high-performance workloads requiring low-latency storage.

Storage Account Endpoints: Accessing Your Data

Storage account endpoints are the entry points for accessing data stored in Azure Storage. Understanding these endpoints is crucial for seamless data access.

Storage Account Endpoints:

Blob Service Endpoint: Discover the Blob Service endpoint for accessing Azure Blob Storage.

File Service Endpoint: Explore the File Service endpoint for Azure File Storage.

Queue Service Endpoint: Understand the Queue Service endpoint for Azure Queue Storage.

Table Service Endpoint: Learn about the Table Service endpoint for Azure Table Storage.

Azure Blob Storage: Storing Unstructured Data

Azure Blob Storage is a versatile service for storing unstructured object data. It is the foundation for a wide range of Azure services and solutions.

Key Concepts of Azure Blob Storage:

Containers and Blobs: Understand the concepts of containers and blobs within Azure Blob Storage and their use in organizing and storing data.

Access Tiers: Explore the access tiers available in Azure Blob Storage, including hot, cool, and archive tiers, and their pricing considerations.

Lifecycle Management: Grasp how to manage the lifecycle of data in Azure Blob Storage, including setting retention policies and automating data movement between tiers.

Storage Security: Protecting Your Data

Ensuring data security in Azure Storage is of paramount importance. Azure provides a range of security features and best practices to safeguard your data.

Storage Security Considerations:

Authentication and Authorization: Implement authentication and authorization mechanisms to control access to storage resources.

Shared Access Signatures (SAS): Utilize Shared Access Signatures for granting limited access rights to specific storage resources.

Encryption: Understand data encryption options, including server-side encryption and client-side encryption, to protect data at rest and in transit.

Azure Files and File Sync: File Sharing and Synchronization

Azure Files and Azure File Sync offer solutions for file sharing and synchronization between on-premises environments and the cloud.

Key Aspects of Azure Files and File Sync:

Azure Files: Explore Azure Files for creating file shares and mounting them on Windows, Linux, or macOS devices.

Azure File Sync: Understand how Azure File Sync enables file synchronization between on-premises file servers and Azure File shares.

Managing Storage: Administration and Governance

Effective management of Azure Storage resources is essential for optimizing costs, ensuring data compliance, and maintaining operational efficiency.

Storage Management Considerations:

Monitoring and Metrics: Implement monitoring and utilize metrics to gain insights into the performance and health of your storage resources.

Cost Optimization: Utilize cost management tools and practices to control and optimize storage costs.

Governance and Compliance: Implement governance policies and compliance standards to ensure data integrity, security, and regulatory compliance.

Azure Storage is a vital component of the Azure cloud ecosystem, serving as the foundation for data storage and access in a wide range of Azure services and solutions. Understanding the intricacies of Azure Storage Accounts, the various storage services, replication options, storage account types, storage endpoints, Azure Blob Storage, security considerations, Azure Files, and management best practices is essential for cloud administrators, architects, and data engineers. This knowledge empowers organizations to leverage Azure Storage to its full potential, ensuring data availability, security, and performance while enabling digital transformation and data-driven decision-making.

Exam Essentials for Azure Storage

As you prepare for Microsoft Azure certification exams, including the Microsoft Certified: Azure Administrator Associate (AZ-104) or those focusing on Azure Storage, it's crucial to master the key concepts and best practices related to efficiently managing and securing data storage in Azure. These exam essentials will help you demonstrate your expertise in Azure Storage, including storage accounts, services, security, and management.

1. Azure Storage Accounts

Storage Account Types: Understand the different types of storage accounts, including General Purpose v2, General Purpose v1, Blob Storage, and Premium. Learn how to select the right account type for specific use cases.

Replication Options: Comprehend the purpose and characteristics of storage replication options, such as Locally Redundant Storage (LRS), Geo-Redundant Storage (GRS), Zone-Redundant Storage (ZRS), and Read-Access Geo-Redundant Storage (RA-GRS).

Access Control: Know how to configure access control and permissions for storage accounts, including managing shared access signatures (SAS) for secure data access.

2. Azure Storage Services

Azure Blob Storage: Familiarize yourself with Azure Blob Storage, its use for storing unstructured object data, and the concepts of containers and blobs.

Azure Table Storage: Learn about Azure Table Storage for semi-structured data storage, and understand how it serves as a NoSQL data store for applications.

Azure Queue Storage: Explore Azure Queue Storage and its role in facilitating messaging between application components for asynchronous communication.

Azure File Storage: Understand Azure File Storage for file-based sharing and its use in providing file shares accessible from multiple virtual machines.

3. Storage Replication

Data Redundancy: Understand the importance of data redundancy and replication options to ensure data availability and durability in Azure Storage.

Locally Redundant Storage (LRS): Know the characteristics and use cases of LRS for replicating data within a storage scale unit.

Geo-Redundant Storage (GRS): Learn about GRS, which replicates data to a secondary Azure region for data recovery in case of regional failures.

Zone-Redundant Storage (ZRS): Grasp the concept of ZRS, which replicates data across availability zones within a region for high availability.

Read-Access Geo-Redundant Storage (RA-GRS): Understand RA-GRS, which extends GRS by providing read access to the secondary region.

4. Storage Security

Authentication and Authorization: Implement secure authentication and authorization mechanisms to control access to storage resources and ensure data security.

Shared Access Signatures (SAS): Learn how to use Shared Access Signatures (SAS) for granting limited and secure access rights to specific storage resources.

Encryption: Understand data encryption options, including server-side and client-side encryption, to protect data at rest and in transit.

5. Azure Files and File Sync

Azure Files: Explore Azure Files and how to create file shares and mount them on Windows, Linux, or macOS devices for easy file sharing.

Azure File Sync: Grasp the role of Azure File Sync in enabling file synchronization between on-premises file servers and Azure File shares.

6. Managing Storage

Monitoring and Metrics: Implement monitoring solutions and leverage metrics to gain insights into the performance and health of your storage resources.

Cost Optimization: Utilize cost management tools and practices to control and optimize storage costs, ensuring cost-effective storage solutions.

Governance and Compliance: Implement governance policies and compliance standards to maintain data integrity, security, and regulatory compliance within your storage environment.

By focusing on these exam essentials for Azure Storage, you'll be well-prepared to demonstrate your proficiency in Azure storage management, which is essential for various Azure certifications and roles. Practical experience, hands-on labs, and real-world practice with Azure storage solutions will further solidify your knowledge and skills. These essentials not only aid in exam success but also enable you to effectively design, manage, and secure storage solutions in Azure, supporting your organization's data storage and retrieval requirements.

Review Questions And Answers

Question 1:

What is the primary purpose of Azure Availability Zones?

A. To optimize traffic routing

B. To provide data center redundancy within a region

C. To distribute load-balanced traffic

D. To route traffic to the closest instance

Answer: B. To provide data center redundancy within a region

Question 2:

Which Azure Storage service is designed for storing unstructured object data, such as documents and media files?

A. Azure Queue Storage

B. Azure Table Storage

C. Azure Blob Storage

D. Azure File Storage

Answer: C. Azure Blob Storage

Question 3:

Which Azure Storage replication option replicates data within a storage scale unit for high availability?

A. Geo-Redundant Storage (GRS)

B. Locally Redundant Storage (LRS)

C. Zone-Redundant Storage (ZRS)

D. Read-Access Geo-Redundant Storage (RA-GRS)

Answer: B. Locally Redundant Storage (LRS)

Question 4:

What is the primary use case for Azure Table Storage?

A. Storing structured relational data

B. Storing unstructured object data

C. Storing semi-structured data

D. Storing backups and archives

Answer: C. Storing semi-structured data

Question 5:

Azure File Sync enables synchronization between on-premises file servers and which Azure storage service?

A. Azure Queue Storage

B. Azure Table Storage

C. Azure Blob Storage

D. Azure File Storage

Answer: D. Azure File Storage

Question 6:

Which Azure Storage service is designed for facilitating messaging between application components for asynchronous communication?

A. Azure Table Storage

B. Azure Queue Storage

C. Azure Blob Storage

D. Azure File Storage

Answer: B. Azure Queue Storage

Question 7:

What is the main purpose of Shared Access Signatures (SAS) in Azure Storage?

A. Data encryption at rest

B. Secure authentication and authorization

C. Optimizing data access speed

D. Data access monitoring

Answer: B. Secure authentication and authorization

Question 8:

Which Azure Storage replication option extends Geo-Redundant Storage (GRS) by providing read access to the secondary region?

A. Locally Redundant Storage (LRS)

B. Zone-Redundant Storage (ZRS)

C. Read-Access Geo-Redundant Storage (RA-GRS)

D. Hot Access Tier

Answer: C. Read-Access Geo-Redundant Storage (RA-GRS)

Question 9:

What is the access tier in Azure Blob Storage that is optimized for frequently accessed data?

A. Cool Access Tier

B. Hot Access Tier

C. Archive Access Tier

D. General Purpose v2

Answer: B. Hot Access Tier

Question 10:

Which storage account type offers a balance of capacity, transaction rates, and pricing for a wide range of workloads?

A. General Purpose v1

B. Premium

C. Blob Storage

D. General Purpose v2

Answer: D. General Purpose v2

Question 11:

Which Azure Storage service is used for NoSQL data storage and provides a key/ attribute store with a schemaless design?

A. Azure Blob Storage

B. Azure Table Storage

C. Azure Queue Storage

D. Azure File Storage

Answer: B. Azure Table Storage

Question 12:

What is the purpose of Azure File Storage?

A. Storing unstructured object data

B. Storing backups and archives

C. File-based sharing and access from multiple virtual machines

D. Facilitating messaging between application components

Answer: C. File-based sharing and access from multiple virtual machines

Question 13:

Which Azure Storage service is used for file-based sharing and synchronization between on-premises file servers and the cloud?

A. Azure File Sync

B. Azure Blob Storage

C. Azure Queue Storage

D. Azure Table Storage

Answer: A. Azure File Sync

Question 14:

Which Azure Storage replication option replicates data to a secondary Azure region for data recovery in case of regional failures?

A. Locally Redundant Storage (LRS)

B. Geo-Redundant Storage (GRS)

C. Zone-Redundant Storage (ZRS)

D. Read-Access Geo-Redundant Storage (RA-GRS)

Answer: B. Geo-Redundant Storage (GRS)

Question 15:

What are the access tiers available in Azure Blob Storage?

A. Hot, Cold, and Archive

B. Basic, Standard, and Premium

C. Fast, Medium, and Slow

D. Free, Trial, and Paid

Answer: A. Hot, Cold, and Archive

Question 16:

Which Azure Storage service is designed for storing structured relational data?

A. Azure Blob Storage

B. Azure Table Storage

C. Azure Queue Storage

D. Azure File Storage

Answer: Not Applicable. None of the options are applicable for structured relational data storage.

Question 17:

What is the primary role of Azure Blob Storage containers?

A. Storing backups and archives

B. Organizing and storing data

C. Facilitating messaging between application components

D. Providing shared access to virtual machines

Answer: B. Organizing and storing data

Question 18:

Which Azure Storage service is used for creating file shares and mounting them on Windows, Linux, or macOS devices?

A. Azure Blob Storage

B. Azure Table Storage

C. Azure Queue Storage

D. Azure File Storage

Answer: D. Azure File Storage

Question 19:

What is the purpose of Azure File Sync in hybrid cloud environments?

A. Data encryption at rest

B. Synchronizing on-premises file servers with Azure File shares

C. Secure authentication and authorization

D. Optimizing data access speed

Answer: B. Synchronizing on-premises file servers with Azure File shares

Question 20:

Which Azure Storage service provides a key/attribute store with a schemaless design?

A. Azure Blob Storage

B. Azure Table Storage

C. Azure Queue Storage

D. Azure File Storage

Answer: B. Azure Table Storage

Question 21:

What is the primary use case for Azure Queue Storage?

A. Storing backups and archives

B. Synchronizing on-premises file servers

C. Facilitating messaging between application components

D. Data encryption at rest

Answer: C. Facilitating messaging between application components

Question 22:

Which access tier in Azure Blob Storage is optimized for infrequently accessed data at a lower storage cost?

A. Hot Access Tier

B. Cool Access Tier

C. Archive Access Tier

D. General Purpose v2

Answer: B. Cool Access Tier

Question 23:

What is the primary benefit of using Shared Access Signatures (SAS) in Azure Storage?

A. Data encryption at rest

B. Secure authentication and authorization

C. Optimizing data access speed

D. Data access monitoring

Answer: B. Secure authentication and authorization

Question 24:

Which Azure Storage replication option replicates data across availability zones within a region to ensure high availability?

A. Locally Redundant Storage (LRS)

B. Geo-Redundant Storage (GRS)

C. Zone-Redundant Storage (ZRS)

D. Read-Access Geo-Redundant Storage (RA-GRS)

Answer: C. Zone-Redundant Storage (ZRS)

Question 25:

What is the purpose of Azure File Storage?

A. Storing unstructured object data

B. Storing backups and archives

C. File-based sharing and access from multiple virtual machines

D. Facilitating messaging between application components

Answer: C. File-based sharing and access from multiple virtual machines

Question 26:

Which Azure Storage service is used for NoSQL data storage and provides a key/attribute store with a schemaless design?

A. Azure Blob Storage

B. Azure Table Storage

C. Azure Queue Storage

D. Azure File Storage

Answer: B. Azure Table Storage

Question 27:

What is the primary role of Azure Blob Storage containers?

A. Storing backups and archives

B. Organizing and storing data

C. Facilitating messaging between application components

D. Providing shared access to virtual machines

Answer: B. Organizing and storing data

Question 28:

Which Azure Storage service is used for creating file shares and mounting them on Windows, Linux, or macOS devices?

A. Azure Blob Storage

B. Azure Table Storage

C. Azure Queue Storage

D. Azure File Storage

Answer: D. Azure File Storage

Question 29:

What is the primary benefit of using Shared Access Signatures (SAS) in Azure Storage?

A. Data encryption at rest

B. Secure authentication and authorization

C. Optimizing data access speed

D. Data access monitoring

Answer: B. Secure authentication and authorization

Question 30:

Which access tier in Azure Blob Storage is optimized for infrequently accessed data at a lower storage cost?

A. Hot Access Tier

B. Cool Access Tier

C. Archive Access Tier

D. General Purpose v2

Answer: B. Cool Access Tier

Chapter 7: Azure Virtual Machines

Azure Virtual Machines (VMs) stand as the cornerstone of Microsoft Azure's Infrastructure as a Service (IaaS) offerings. They provide unparalleled flexibility, scalability, and control over your cloud resources. In this chapter, we will explore the essential aspects of Azure Virtual Machines, including planning, deployment, connectivity, high availability, scaling, and the concept of Virtual Machine Scale Sets.

Virtual Machine Planning

Before delving into the deployment of Azure Virtual Machines, it is crucial to start with comprehensive planning. This phase involves defining the needs, specifications, and requirements of your VMs. Key aspects of VM planning include:

Resource Sizing: Determine the appropriate size and configuration of your VMs based on CPU, memory, and storage requirements.

Operating System Selection: Choose the operating system that best suits your applications, workloads, and compliance requirements. Azure supports various Windows and Linux distributions.

Networking and Security: Plan the network architecture, including subnets, virtual networks, and security groups, to ensure proper isolation and connectivity.

Data Disposition: Decide how you will manage data, including data storage, backups, and disaster recovery.

Licensing: Address licensing considerations for your chosen operating systems and any software applications running on the VMs.

Deploying Virtual Machines

Once your VM planning is complete, it's time to deploy Virtual Machines. Azure offers multiple methods for VM deployment:

Azure Portal: The web-based Azure Portal provides an intuitive interface for creating VMs, including selecting pre-configured templates and specifying custom settings.

Azure CLI: The Azure Command-Line Interface allows for script-based VM deployment and automation.

Azure PowerShell: Azure PowerShell modules provide extensive capabilities for scripting VM creation and management.

ARM Templates: Azure Resource Manager (ARM) templates offer a way to define infrastructure as code, enabling consistent and repeatable VM deployments.

Azure Marketplace: You can choose from a variety of pre-configured VM images from the Azure Marketplace for different use cases, such as web hosting, databases, or development.

Connecting to Virtual Machines

After deploying VMs, it's essential to establish connectivity for management and application access. This involves:

Remote Desktop Protocol (RDP): For Windows VMs, you can use RDP to connect remotely. Ensure that network security groups allow RDP traffic.

SSH (Secure Shell): For Linux VMs, SSH is the standard protocol for remote access. Be sure to secure SSH access with keys or passwords.

Azure Bastion: Azure Bastion is a managed service that provides secure and seamless RDP and SSH access to VMs without exposing them to the public internet.

Azure VPN Gateway: To create a secure connection between on-premises networks and Azure VMs, Azure VPN Gateway is used.

Availability of Virtual Machines

High availability is a crucial consideration when planning your VM deployment. Azure offers multiple options to ensure your VMs remain accessible:

Availability Sets: Place VMs in an availability set to distribute them across multiple fault domains and update domains. This provides resilience against hardware failures and planned maintenance events.

Availability Zones: Azure regions with availability zones offer even greater redundancy. VMs in different availability zones remain operational even if an entire data center becomes unavailable.

Virtual Machine Scale Sets: These automatically distribute VM instances across multiple fault domains, ensuring high availability and scalability.

Scaling Concepts

Azure Virtual Machines are designed to be flexible and scalable. There are two primary scaling concepts to consider:

Vertical Scaling (Scaling Up/Down): Involves changing the VM size by increasing or decreasing CPU and memory resources. This is useful for handling varying workloads and optimizing costs.

Horizontal Scaling (Scaling Out/In): Involves adding or removing VM instances to accommodate varying workloads. This approach is ideal for distributing load and achieving high availability.

Virtual Machine Scale Sets

Virtual Machine Scale Sets (VMSS) simplify the management of a group of identical VMs. Key features and considerations for VMSS include:

Auto Scaling: VMSS can automatically adjust the number of VM instances based on performance metrics or a predefined schedule.

Load Balancing: VMSS instances are automatically load balanced to ensure even distribution of traffic.

Custom Images: You can use custom images to deploy VMSS instances, allowing for consistent configurations and easy updates.

Rolling Upgrades: VMSS supports rolling upgrades, ensuring zero-downtime updates for your application.

Health Probes: Define health probes to monitor the state of VM instances and ensure traffic is directed to healthy instances.

Integration with Azure Services: VMSS can be integrated with Azure services like Azure DevOps for automated deployment and scaling.

In conclusion, Azure Virtual Machines offer unparalleled flexibility and control over your cloud infrastructure. Effective planning, deployment, connectivity, high availability, and scalability are essential aspects to master when working with Azure VMs. Whether you are a cloud administrator, developer, or architect, understanding these concepts is crucial for building reliable and scalable solutions in the Azure cloud environment. With the knowledge gained from this chapter, you can harness the power of Azure VMs to meet your organization's computing needs while optimizing cost and performance.

Exam Essentials for Azure Virtual Machines

As you prepare for Microsoft Azure certification exams, including the Microsoft Certified: Azure Administrator Associate (AZ-104) or other Azure-related certifications, mastering the essentials of Azure Virtual Machines (VMs) is critical. These exam essentials will help you demonstrate your proficiency in planning, deploying, managing, and optimizing Azure VMs.

1. Virtual Machine Planning

Resource Sizing: Understand how to determine the appropriate size and configuration of VMs based on CPU, memory, and storage requirements for specific workloads.

Operating System Selection: Familiarize yourself with the process of selecting the right operating system for your VMs, considering factors like application compatibility and compliance.

Networking and Security: Learn to plan the network architecture, including virtual networks, subnets, and security groups, to ensure secure and efficient VM communication.

Data Disposition: Comprehend the strategies for managing data, including data storage, backups, and disaster recovery.

Licensing: Understand licensing considerations for VMs, including licensing for the chosen operating system and any additional software applications.

2. Deploying Virtual Machines

Azure Portal: Be prepared to create VMs through the Azure Portal, using pre-configured templates or custom settings.

Azure CLI and Azure PowerShell: Gain familiarity with deploying VMs via command-line interfaces, enabling script-based deployments and automation.

ARM Templates: Learn how to use Azure Resource Manager (ARM) templates to define infrastructure as code, ensuring consistent and repeatable VM deployments.

Azure Marketplace: Know how to choose and deploy pre-configured VM images from the Azure Marketplace to meet various use cases.

3. Connecting to Virtual Machines

RDP and SSH: Understand the processes for connecting to Windows VMs using Remote Desktop Protocol (RDP) and to Linux VMs using Secure Shell (SSH).

Azure Bastion: Be aware of Azure Bastion as a managed service for secure and seamless RDP and SSH access to VMs without exposing them to the public internet.

Azure VPN Gateway: Recognize Azure VPN Gateway as a solution for creating secure connections between on-premises networks and Azure VMs.

4. High Availability of Virtual Machines

Availability Sets: Learn how to place VMs in availability sets to distribute them across multiple fault domains and update domains, ensuring high availability and resilience against hardware failures and maintenance events.

Availability Zones: Understand the concept of availability zones, available in some Azure regions, which provide even greater redundancy by distributing VMs across isolated data centers.

Virtual Machine Scale Sets (VMSS): Familiarize yourself with VMSS, which automatically distributes identical VM instances across multiple fault domains, ensuring high availability and scalability.

5. Scaling Concepts

Vertical Scaling (Scaling Up/Down): Know how to change VM sizes to increase or decrease CPU and memory resources for optimizing performance and cost.

Horizontal Scaling (Scaling Out/In): Understand the concept of adding or removing VM instances to accommodate varying workloads, distribute load, and achieve high availability.

6. Virtual Machine Scale Sets

Auto Scaling: Recognize that VMSS supports auto scaling based on performance metrics or predefined schedules, adjusting the number of VM instances as needed.

Load Balancing: Understand that VMSS instances are automatically load balanced to ensure even distribution of traffic.

Custom Images: Learn to use custom images to deploy VMSS instances, enabling consistent configurations and easy updates.

Rolling Upgrades: Be aware that VMSS supports rolling upgrades, ensuring zero-downtime updates for your application.

Health Probes: Understand the importance of defining health probes to monitor VM instance health and direct traffic to healthy instances.

Integration with Azure Services: Know that VMSS can be integrated with Azure services like Azure DevOps for automated deployment and scaling.

These essentials cover the core topics related to Azure Virtual Machines that you should master when preparing for Azure certification exams and working with VMs in real-world scenarios. Practical experience, hands-on labs, and comprehensive understanding of these concepts will enhance your proficiency in managing Azure VMs effectively.

Review Questions And Answers

Question 1:

What is the primary purpose of Azure Availability Zones?

A. To optimize traffic routing

B. To provide data center redundancy within a region

C. To distribute load-balanced traffic

D. To route traffic to the closest instance

Answer: B. To provide data center redundancy within a region

Question 2:

Which service is used for secure and seamless RDP and SSH access to Azure Virtual Machines?

A. Azure Bastion

B. Azure VPN Gateway

C. Azure Firewall

D. Azure Load Balancer

Answer: A. Azure Bastion

Question 3:

In Azure, what is the primary benefit of placing Virtual Machines in availability sets?

A. Improved network performance

B. Simplified management

C. Data redundancy

D. High availability

Answer: D. High availability

Question 4:

Which Azure service provides a way to define infrastructure as code, ensuring consistent and repeatable VM deployments?

A. Azure CLI

B. Azure Bastion

C. Azure Resource Manager (ARM) templates

D. Azure Virtual Network

Answer: C. Azure Resource Manager (ARM) templates

Question 5:

What is the purpose of Azure Virtual Machine Scale Sets (VMSS)?

A. To enable remote access to VMs

B. To distribute load-balanced traffic

C. To provide data center redundancy

D. To automatically distribute identical VM instances

Answer: D. To automatically distribute identical VM instances

Question 6:

Which scaling concept involves changing the size and configuration of VMs to optimize performance and cost?

A. Horizontal Scaling

B. Vertical Scaling

C. Availability Scaling

D. Elastic Scaling

Answer: B. Vertical Scaling

Question 7:

Azure Virtual Machines support which of the following operating systems? (Select all that apply)

A. Windows

B. Linux

C. macOS

D. Android

Answer: A. Windows, B. Linux

Question 8:

What Azure service is used for creating secure connections between on-premises networks and Azure VMs?

A. Azure Bastion

B. Azure VPN Gateway

C. Azure Firewall

D. Azure Load Balancer

Answer: B. Azure VPN Gateway

Question 9:

Which Azure scaling concept involves adding or removing VM instances to accommodate varying workloads?

A. Vertical Scaling

B. Horizontal Scaling

C. Elastic Scaling

D. Availability Scaling

Answer: B. Horizontal Scaling

Question 10:

Which Azure Virtual Machine deployment method allows for consistent and repeatable deployments through infrastructure as code?

A. Azure Portal

B. Azure CLI

C. Azure PowerShell

D. ARM Templates

Answer: D. ARM Templates

Question 11:

What is the primary benefit of using Azure Bastion for remote access to VMs?

A. It allows public internet access to VMs.

B. It ensures secure and seamless RDP and SSH access to VMs.

C. It provides load balancing for VMs.

D. It offers data center redundancy.

Answer: B. It ensures secure and seamless RDP and SSH access to VMs.

Question 12:

Which Azure Virtual Machine concept involves automatically adjusting the number of VM instances based on performance metrics or a predefined schedule?

A. Availability Sets

B. Availability Zones

C. Vertical Scaling

D. Virtual Machine Scale Sets

Answer: D. Virtual Machine Scale Sets

Question 13:

Which Azure service is used for secure and seamless RDP and SSH access to Azure Virtual Machines?

A. Azure Bastion

B. Azure VPN Gateway

C. Azure Firewall

D. Azure Load Balancer

Answer: A. Azure Bastion

Question 14:

What is the primary purpose of Availability Zones in Azure?

A. To optimize traffic routing

B. To provide data center redundancy within a region

C. To distribute load-balanced traffic

D. To route traffic to the closest instance

Answer: B. To provide data center redundancy within a region

Question 15:

In Azure, what is the primary benefit of placing Virtual Machines in availability sets?

A. Improved network performance

B. Simplified management

C. Data redundancy

D. High availability

Answer: D. High availability

Question 16:

Which Azure service provides a way to define infrastructure as code, ensuring consistent and repeatable VM deployments?

A. Azure CLI

B. Azure Bastion

C. Azure Resource Manager (ARM) templates

D. Azure Virtual Network

Answer: C. Azure Resource Manager (ARM) templates

Question 17:

What is the purpose of Azure Virtual Machine Scale Sets (VMSS)?

A. To enable remote access to VMs

B. To distribute load-balanced traffic

C. To provide data center redundancy

D. To automatically distribute identical VM instances

Answer: D. To automatically distribute identical VM instances

Question 18:

Which scaling concept involves changing the size and configuration of VMs to optimize performance and cost?

A. Horizontal Scaling

B. Vertical Scaling

C. Availability Scaling

D. Elastic Scaling

Answer: B. Vertical Scaling

Question 19:

Azure Virtual Machines support which of the following operating systems? (Select all that apply)

A. Windows

B. Linux

C. macOS

D. Android

Answer: A. Windows, B. Linux

Question 20:

What Azure service is used for creating secure connections between on-premises networks and Azure VMs?

A. Azure Bastion

B. Azure VPN Gateway

C. Azure Firewall

D. Azure Load Balancer

Answer: B. Azure VPN Gateway

Question 21:

Which Azure scaling concept involves adding or removing VM instances to accommodate varying workloads?

A. Vertical Scaling

B. Horizontal Scaling

C. Elastic Scaling

D. Availability Scaling

Answer: B. Horizontal Scaling

Question 22:

Which Azure Virtual Machine deployment method allows for consistent and repeatable deployments through infrastructure as code?

A. Azure Portal

B. Azure CLI

C. Azure PowerShell

D. ARM Templates

Answer: D. ARM Templates

Chapter 8: Automation, Deployment, and Configuration of Resources

In the ever-evolving landscape of cloud computing, automation and efficient resource management are pivotal. Azure, Microsoft's cloud platform, provides a robust set of tools and services to streamline the deployment and configuration of resources. This chapter delves into essential aspects of Azure Resource Manager, ARM Templates, configuring virtual hard disk templates, and utilizing virtual machine extensions.

Azure Resource Manager (ARM)

Azure Resource Manager is the orchestration service used to deploy and manage resources in an Azure subscription. Its core benefits include:

Resource Group Management: ARM enables you to organize related resources into resource groups for unified management, billing, and monitoring.

Deployment Templates: ARM templates allow you to define your infrastructure as code, providing a blueprint for resource deployment.

Role-Based Access Control (RBAC): ARM integrates RBAC to control access and permissions for resources, promoting security and governance.

Resource Locks: Utilize resource locks to prevent accidental deletion or modification of critical resources.

Tagging: Apply tags to resources for efficient categorization, monitoring, and cost management.

ARM Templates

Azure Resource Manager Templates, commonly referred to as ARM templates, are JSON-based files used for declarative resource deployment. Key components and concepts of ARM templates include:

Resource Definitions: Templates define the Azure resources you want to deploy, specifying properties like resource type, location, and dependencies.

Parameters: Use parameters to make templates flexible and reusable, allowing customization during deployment.

Variables: Define variables for reusing expressions within the template, enhancing readability and maintainability.

Outputs: Outputs provide information about deployed resources, facilitating integration with external systems.

Conditions and Loops: Employ conditions and loops to implement complex control flow and resource creation logic.

Configuring Virtual Hard Disk Templates

Configuring virtual hard disk (VHD) templates is a critical component of resource deployment and management. It involves the following considerations:

Customization: Customize base OS images with specific configurations, software, and settings to meet your application's requirements.

Image Capture: After customization, capture the virtual machine as a generalized VHD image to be used for deployment.

Managed Images: Store VHD templates as managed images in Azure for versioning, scalability, and accessibility.

Gallery Images: Publish VHD templates as gallery images, allowing easy sharing with others and integration into Azure Marketplace.

Virtual Machine Extensions

Azure virtual machine extensions are small applications that provide post-deployment configuration, automation, and maintenance. Essential aspects of virtual machine extensions include:

Built-In Extensions: Azure offers a variety of built-in extensions for tasks like custom script execution, diagnostics, and anti-malware.

Custom Script Extensions: Use custom script extensions to run scripts on VMs for application-specific configuration.

VM Agent: The Azure VM Agent facilitates communication with extensions and helps manage VM health and updates.

Configuration Drift Detection: VM extensions help detect and remediate configuration drift, ensuring VM compliance with desired settings.

Diagnostics and Monitoring: Leverage extensions for diagnostics and monitoring to gain insights into VM performance and health.

Automation, deployment, and configuration of resources are fundamental to efficiently managing cloud infrastructure. Azure Resource Manager, ARM templates, virtual hard disk templates, and virtual machine extensions are powerful tools and concepts that enable streamlined, repeatable, and manageable resource deployments in Microsoft Azure. By mastering these elements, cloud administrators, developers, and architects can optimize resource utilization, enhance security, and ensure scalability in the Azure environment.

Exam Essentials for Automation, Deployment, and Configuration of Resources in Azure

As you prepare for Microsoft Azure certification exams, including the Microsoft Certified: Azure Administrator Associate (AZ-104) or other Azure-related certifications, understanding the essentials of automation, deployment, and configuration of resources is crucial. These exam essentials will help you demonstrate your proficiency in managing Azure resources efficiently.

1. Azure Resource Manager (ARM)

Resource Group Management: Learn how to create, manage, and organize resources within Azure resource groups to enhance management, billing, and monitoring.

Deployment Templates: Understand the concept of ARM templates, which define your infrastructure as code, providing a blueprint for resource deployment.

Role-Based Access Control (RBAC): Be familiar with RBAC, as it allows you to control access and permissions for Azure resources, ensuring security and governance.

Resource Locks: Comprehend how resource locks can be used to prevent accidental deletion or modification of critical resources.

Tagging: Explore the use of tags to categorize and label resources for efficient tracking, monitoring, and cost management.

2. ARM Templates

Resource Definitions: Master the creation of ARM templates that define the Azure resources you want to deploy, specifying their properties and relationships.

Parameters: Understand the role of parameters in making ARM templates flexible and customizable during resource deployment.

Variables: Learn how to define and use variables to enhance the readability and maintainability of ARM templates.

Outputs: Explore the use of outputs to extract information about deployed resources, facilitating integration with external systems.

Conditions and Loops: Gain proficiency in employing conditions and loops within ARM templates to implement complex control flow and resource creation logic.

3. Configuring Virtual Hard Disk Templates

Customization: Know how to customize base OS images to include specific configurations, software, and settings that meet your application's requirements.

Image Capture: Learn the process of capturing a virtual machine as a generalized VHD image to be used as a template for resource deployment.

Managed Images: Understand the benefits of storing VHD templates as managed images in Azure, allowing for versioning, scalability, and accessibility.

Gallery Images: Explore the steps to publish VHD templates as gallery images, making them shareable and integrable with Azure Marketplace.

4. Virtual Machine Extensions

Built-In Extensions: Be aware of the various built-in extensions available in Azure, such as custom script execution, diagnostics, and anti-malware, for post-deployment configuration and automation.

Custom Script Extensions: Know how to use custom script extensions to execute custom scripts on virtual machines for application-specific configuration.

VM Agent: Understand the role of the Azure VM Agent in facilitating communication with extensions and managing VM health and updates.

Configuration Drift Detection: Learn how VM extensions help detect and remediate configuration drift to maintain VM compliance with desired settings.

Diagnostics and Monitoring: Explore how extensions can be leveraged for diagnostics and monitoring, providing insights into VM performance and health.

By mastering these exam essentials, you will be well-equipped to demonstrate your proficiency in automation, deployment, and configuration of resources within Azure, a skill set that is highly valuable for cloud administrators, developers, and architects working in Azure environments.

Review Questions and Answers

Question 1:

What is the primary function of Azure Resource Manager (ARM) in Azure?

A. To create virtual machines

B. To deploy and manage resources

C. To manage cloud billing

D. To provide network security

Answer: B. To deploy and manage resources

Question 2:

What is the main benefit of using Azure Resource Manager templates (ARM templates)?

A. Simplifying Azure billing

B. Defining infrastructure as code for resource deployment

C. Providing direct access to virtual machines

D. Automating Azure Backup

Answer: B. Defining infrastructure as code for resource deployment

Question 3:

Which component of ARM templates allows for customization during deployment?

A. Resource definitions

B. Parameters

C. Variables

D. Outputs

Answer: B. Parameters

Question 4:

What is the primary purpose of Azure Resource Group Management?

A. To organize related resources for unified management, billing, and monitoring

B. To provide secure access to virtual machines

C. To configure virtual networks

D. To monitor network traffic

Answer: A. To organize related resources for unified management, billing, and monitoring

Question 5:

What is the primary function of role-based access control (RBAC) in Azure Resource Manager?

A. To manage VM extensions

B. To control access and permissions for resources

C. To create virtual networks

D. To automate resource deployment

Answer: B. To control access and permissions for resources

Question 6:

What is the purpose of Azure Resource Locks?

A. To prevent accidental deletion or modification of critical resources

B. To optimize traffic routing

C. To distribute load-balanced traffic

D. To route traffic to the closest instance

Answer: A. To prevent accidental deletion or modification of critical resources

Question 7:

Which component of ARM templates is used for defining the desired state of deployed resources?

A. Parameters

B. Variables

C. Resource definitions

D. Outputs

Answer: C. Resource definitions

Question 8:

What is the primary advantage of using tags in Azure?

A. To optimize performance of virtual machines

B. To categorize and label resources for efficient tracking, monitoring, and cost management

C. To improve VM security

D. To create virtual networks

Answer: B. To categorize and label resources for efficient tracking, monitoring, and cost management

Question 9:

Which resource management concept in Azure involves organizing related resources into a single unit for management and billing?

A. Role-Based Access Control (RBAC)

B. Azure Resource Manager (ARM)

C. Resource Group Management

D. Virtual Machine Extensions

Answer: C. Resource Group Management

Question 10:

In Azure, what are role-based access control (RBAC) roles used for?

A. Automating virtual machine deployment

B. Managing Azure Resource Groups

C. Controlling access and permissions for resources

D. Diagnosing VM performance issues

Answer: C. Controlling access and permissions for resources

Question 11:

What is the purpose of Azure Resource Locks?

A. To optimize traffic routing

B. To prevent accidental deletion or modification of critical resources

C. To distribute load-balanced traffic

D. To route traffic to the closest instance

Answer: B. To prevent accidental deletion or modification of critical resources

Question 12:

What is the primary role of variables in ARM templates?

A. To define the infrastructure as code

B. To specify resource dependencies

C. To facilitate customization during deployment

D. To enhance resource security

Answer: C. To facilitate customization during deployment

Question 13:

Which component of ARM templates is used to extract information about deployed resources for integration with external systems?

A. Parameters

B. Variables

C. Resource definitions

D. Outputs

Answer: D. Outputs

Question 14:

In Azure, what does tagging allow you to do?

A. Optimize virtual machine performance

B. Categorize and label resources for efficient tracking and monitoring

C. Manage Azure Resource Groups

D. Automate Azure Backup

Answer: B. Categorize and label resources for efficient tracking and monitoring

Question 15:

What are parameters used for in ARM templates?

A. To customize resources during deployment

B. To extract information about deployed resources

C. To define resource types

D. To specify dependencies between resources

Answer: A. To customize resources during deployment

Question 16:

Which component of ARM templates allows you to extract information about deployed resources for integration with external systems?

A. Parameters

B. Variables

C. Resource definitions

D. Outputs

Answer: D. Outputs

Question 17:

In Azure, what is the purpose of capturing a virtual machine as a generalized VHD image?

A. To create a new virtual machine

B. To take a snapshot of the VM's current state

C. To generate a backup of the VM

D. To create a template for resource deployment

Answer: D. To create a template for resource deployment

Question 18:

What is the primary benefit of storing VHD templates as managed images in Azure?

A. To reduce storage costs

B. To improve VM performance

C. To ensure versioning, scalability, and accessibility

D. To simplify role-based access control

Answer: C. To ensure versioning, scalability, and accessibility

Question 19:

What is the primary purpose of publishing VHD templates as gallery images?

A. To reduce VM deployment time

B. To share templates with other Azure users

C. To increase VM security

D. To improve VM performance

Answer: B. To share templates with other Azure users

Question 20:

Which component of ARM templates defines the desired state of deployed resources?

A. Parameters

B. Variables

C. Resource definitions

D. Outputs

Answer: C. Resource definitions

Question 21:

What is the primary purpose of Azure virtual machine extensions?

A. To create virtual networks

B. To provide additional security for virtual machines

C. To manage Azure Resource Groups

D. To facilitate post-deployment configuration and automation

Answer: D. To facilitate post-deployment configuration and automation

Question 22:

Which type of extension is used to execute custom scripts on Azure virtual machines?

A. Built-in extensions

B. Diagnostics extensions

C. Networking extensions

D. Custom script extensions

Answer: D. Custom script extensions

Question 23:

What is the role of the Azure VM Agent in virtual machine extensions?

A. To automate virtual machine deployment

B. To manage VM security

C. To facilitate communication with extensions and manage VM health and updates

D. To optimize virtual machine performance

Answer: C. To facilitate communication with extensions and manage VM health and updates

Question 24:

What is the primary purpose of custom script extensions in Azure?

A. To execute custom scripts on Azure virtual machines for post-deployment configuration

B. To diagnose performance issues on virtual machines

C. To manage virtual machine backups

D. To optimize virtual machine performance

Answer: A. To execute custom scripts on Azure virtual machines for post-deployment configuration

Question 25:

Which Azure extension is commonly used to install anti-malware software on virtual machines?

A. Custom script extensions

B. Networking extensions

C. Security extensions

D. Diagnostics extensions

Answer: C. Security extensions

Question 26:

What is the primary function of the Azure VM Agent?

A. To monitor network traffic

B. To manage VM backups

C. To facilitate communication with extensions and manage VM health and updates

D. To optimize VM performance

Answer: C. To facilitate communication with extensions and manage VM health and updates

Question 27:

Which extension is often used for monitoring and diagnosing virtual machine performance?

A. Custom script extensions

B. Diagnostics extensions

C. Networking extensions

D. Security extensions

Answer: B. Diagnostics extensions

Question 28:

What is the primary purpose of built-in extensions in Azure?

A. To manage virtual machine backups

B. To optimize virtual machine performance

C. To facilitate post-deployment configuration and automation

D. To diagnose virtual machine performance issues

Answer: C. To facilitate post-deployment configuration and automation

Question 29:

In Azure, what is the role of variables in ARM templates?

A. To define resource dependencies

B. To specify the order of resource creation

C. To facilitate customization during deployment

D. To define resource types

Answer: C. To facilitate customization during deployment

Question 30:

What is the primary role of parameters in ARM templates?

A. To define the order of resource creation

B. To specify the type of resources to be created

C. To define resource dependencies

D. To allow for customization during deployment

Answer: D. To allow for customization during deployment

Question 31:

What is the main benefit of ARM templates in Azure?

A. Simplifying Azure billing

B. Defining infrastructure as code for resource deployment

C. Providing direct access to virtual machines

D. Automating Azure Backup

Answer: B. Defining infrastructure as code for resource deployment

Question 32:

What is the primary purpose of Azure Resource Group Management?

A. To optimize virtual machine performance

B. To organize related resources for unified management, billing, and monitoring

C. To configure network security

D. To manage Azure backups

Answer: B. To organize related resources for unified management, billing, and monitoring

Question 33:

What is the role of outputs in ARM templates?

A. To define the order of resource creation

B. To specify the type of resources to be created

C. To extract information about deployed resources for integration with external systems

D. To allow for customization during deployment

Answer: C. To extract information about deployed resources for integration with external systems

Question 34:

What is the primary advantage of using tags in Azure?

A. To create virtual networks

B. To improve VM security

C. To categorize and label resources for efficient tracking, monitoring, and cost management

D. To optimize virtual machine performance

Answer: C. To categorize and label resources for efficient tracking, monitoring, and cost management

Question 35:

Which resource management concept in Azure involves organizing related resources into a single unit for management and billing?

A. Role-Based Access Control (RBAC)

B. Azure Resource Manager (ARM)

C. Resource Group Management

D. Virtual Machine Extensions

Answer: C. Resource Group Management

Question 36:

In Azure, what does role-based access control (RBAC) allow you to do?

A. Automate virtual machine deployment

B. Manage Azure Resource Groups

C. Control access and permissions for resources

D. Diagnose VM performance issues

Answer: C. Control access and permissions for resources

Question 37:

What is the purpose of Azure Resource Locks?

A. To optimize traffic routing

B. To prevent accidental deletion or modification of critical resources

C. To distribute load-balanced traffic

D. To route traffic to the closest instance

Answer: B. To prevent accidental deletion or modification of critical resources

Question 38:

What is the primary role of variables in ARM templates?

A. To define the infrastructure as code

B. To specify resource dependencies

C. To facilitate customization during deployment

D. To enhance resource security

Answer: C. To facilitate customization during deployment

Question 39:

Which component of ARM templates is used to extract information about deployed resources for integration with external systems?

A. Parameters

B. Variables

C. Resource definitions

D. Outputs

Answer: D. Outputs

Question 40:

In Azure, what does tagging allow you to do?

A. Optimize virtual machine performance

B. Categorize and label resources for efficient tracking and monitoring

C. Manage Azure Resource Groups

D. Automate Azure Backup

Answer: B. Categorize and label resources for efficient tracking and monitoring

Question 41:

What are parameters used for in ARM templates?

A. To customize resources during deployment

B. To extract information about deployed resources

C. To define resource types

D. To specify dependencies between resources

Answer: A. To customize resources during deployment

Question 42:

Which component of ARM templates allows you to extract information about deployed resources for integration with external systems?

A. Parameters

B. Variables

C. Resource definitions

D. Outputs

Answer: D. Outputs

Question 43:

In Azure, what is the purpose of capturing a virtual machine as a generalized VHD image?

A. To create a new virtual machine

B. To take a snapshot of the VM's current state

C. To generate a backup of the VM

D. To create a template for resource deployment

Answer: D. To create a template for resource deployment

Question 44:

What is the primary benefit of storing VHD templates as managed images in Azure?

A. To reduce storage costs

B. To improve VM performance

C. To ensure versioning, scalability, and accessibility

D. To simplify role-based access control

Answer: C. To ensure versioning, scalability, and accessibility

Question 45:

What is the primary purpose of publishing VHD templates as gallery images?

A. To reduce VM deployment time

B. To share templates with other Azure users

C. To increase VM security

D. To improve VM performance

Answer: B. To share templates with other Azure users

Question 46:

Which component of ARM templates defines the desired state of deployed resources?

A. Parameters

B. Variables

C. Resource definitions

D. Outputs

Answer: C. Resource definitions

Question 47:

What is the primary purpose of Azure virtual machine extensions?

A. To create virtual networks

B. To provide additional security for virtual machines

C. To manage Azure Resource Groups

D. To facilitate post-deployment configuration and automation

Answer: D. To facilitate post-deployment configuration and automation

Conclusion

obtaining the Microsoft Certified: Azure Administrator Associate certification is a significant achievement that signifies your expertise in managing and maintaining Azure resources. As a certified Azure administrator, you have the knowledge and skills needed to ensure the efficient operation of Azure environments, secure data and applications, and optimize cloud resources for your organization.

This book has provided you with a comprehensive guide to help you prepare for the certification exam. It has covered various essential topics, including Azure Active Directory, compliance and cloud governance, virtual networking, network traffic management, Azure storage, intersite connectivity, and Azure virtual machines, as well as automation, deployment, and configuration of resources. Additionally, you've had the opportunity to test your knowledge with review questions and answers throughout the book.

To further enhance your exam readiness, we've provided a set of practice test questions and answers, simulating real exam scenarios. These questions cover a wide range of topics relevant to the Azure Administrator Associate certification and are designed to challenge your understanding and reinforce your learning.

As you approach the certification exam, here are some key takeaways and tips to keep in mind:

Hands-on Experience: Practical experience is invaluable. Make sure to experiment with Azure services and solutions in a sandbox environment, as it helps solidify your understanding of concepts.

Azure Documentation: The Azure documentation is a valuable resource. Use it to complement your study materials and dive deep into specific topics.

Time Management: During the exam, time management is crucial. Carefully allocate time to each question, and if you're unsure about an answer, mark it for review and move on. You can revisit marked questions later.

Practice Tests: Utilize practice tests like the ones provided in this book to gauge your readiness and identify areas that may need additional study.

Stay Updated: Azure is a dynamic platform, and Microsoft regularly updates its services and features. Be sure to keep up with the latest developments in Azure.

Community and Resources: Join Azure-related communities, forums, and social networks. Engaging with peers and experts can provide valuable insights and support.

Don't Cram: It's better to study consistently over time rather than cramming the night before the exam. Understanding the material deeply is more important than memorization.

Read Questions Carefully: When taking the exam, read each question carefully and ensure you understand what is being asked. Pay attention to any specific details or keywords in the question.

Review and Verify: Before submitting your answers, take a moment to review and verify your responses. Ensure you haven't missed any questions or left any answers incomplete.

The Microsoft Certified: Azure Administrator Associate certification is a testament to your expertise in Azure administration. With this certification, you'll be well-equipped to advance your career and contribute to the success of your organization in the ever-evolving world of cloud computing.

We wish you the best of luck as you embark on your certification journey, and may you successfully pass the exam and excel in your Azure administration endeavors.

www.ingramcontent.com/pod-product-compliance
Lightning Source LLC
LaVergne TN
LVHW082345200926
848481LV00012B/3455
* 9 7 9 8 2 2 3 0 8 7 3 2 8 *